Twitter

Twitter

A Biography

Jean Burgess and Nancy K. Baym

NEW YORK UNIVERSITY PRESS

New York

NEW YORK UNIVERSITY PRESS
New York
www.nyupress.org

First published in paperback in 2022

References to Internet websites (URLs) were accurate at the time of writing. Neither the author nor New York University Press is responsible for URLs that may have expired or changed since the manuscript was prepared.

Library of Congress Cataloging-in-Publication Data
Names: Burgess, Jean (Jean Elizabeth), author. | Baym, Nancy K., author.
Title: Twitter : a biography / Jean Burgess and Nancy K. Baym.
Description: New York : New York University Press, [2020] |
Includes bibliographical references and index.
Identifiers: LCCN 2019039539 | ISBN 9781479811069 (cloth) |
ISBN 9781479801756 (paper) | ISBN 9781479823833 (ebook) |
ISBN 9781479841806 (ebook)
Subjects: LCSH: Twitter. | Twitter (Firm)—History. | Online social networks.
Classification: LCC HM743.T95 B87 2020 | DDC 302.30285—dc23
LC record available at https://lccn.loc.gov/2019039539

New York University Press books are printed on acid-free paper, and their binding materials are chosen for strength and durability. We strive to use environmentally responsible suppliers and materials to the greatest extent possible in publishing our books.

Manufactured in the United States of America

10 9 8 7 6 5 4 3 2 1

Also available as an ebook

Contents

Introduction

In 2016, Twitter turned 10. By the middle of that year it was claiming 313 million monthly active users, 82% of whom were using the platform on mobile devices. It had 3,860 employees, 35+ offices around the world, 79% non-US accounts, 40+ supported languages, and one billion unique visits monthly to sites where tweets are embedded.[1] Although it was founded in the US, Twitter is very international, with large and active populations of users outside the English-speaking world including in Japan, India, Indonesia, and Brazil—and even to an extent in China, where the service is officially blocked.

In August 2018, the word "Twitter" appeared in the title of approximately 61,300 of the academic articles listed by Google Scholar,[2] and it had been the principal subject of at least two scholarly books, with the number of publications still growing strongly.[3] Twitter has been described as a "nervous system for the planet" and a "global newsroom," hosting large amounts of

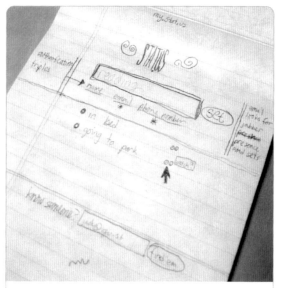

Figure I.1. Concept sketch for a status update–based social network by Jack Dorsey, 2006.

real-time data about social behavior and public communication. It has become the go-to site for journalists seeking to follow the flow of news. Its offering of massive amounts of tweets that can be computationally scraped and analyzed has given rise to whole new fields of social science and humanities research. Many journalists, academics, and politicians are virtually dependent on it as a social listening, professional dialogue, and public relations tool,[4] and it is widely considered an essential component of civic infrastructure for emergency communication.[5] The sense that Twitter matters to the world in such significant ways stands in marked contrast to its far more humble, mundane, and intimate beginnings.

Twitter was officially launched in July 2006. In its earliest incarnation, it was a very lightweight service for updating your friends about your whereabouts, thoughts, or everyday activities—as the early concept drawing for a "status" service by Jack Dorsey shows (see fig I.1). Its original intent, in other words, was to be of importance on an interpersonal rather than geopolitical scale. Before it was even called "Twitter," let alone had its own company, the idea for the service was developed as a side project within Odeo, a startup focused on podcasting products. Its first version could be used through a website initially registered as twttr.com (see fig. I.2), which displayed all updates from all users in one public timeline and (in the US) via SMS on mobile phones—hence its original and once-defining limitation of 140 characters (leaving a buffer of 20 inside the hard limit of 160 characters per SMS).

Twitter had its effective coming-out party at the South by Southwest (SXSW) conference and music festival in March 2007,

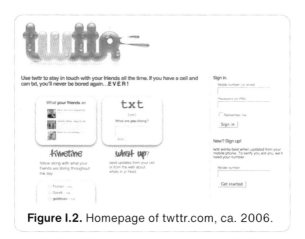

Figure I.2. Homepage of twttr.com, ca. 2006.

where it cemented its place as the social networking site of choice for the influencers of the predominantly white, educated, and urban US technology community. At the conference, Twitter created buzz and encouraged use of their product by displaying live tweets from the event on plasma screens in the hallways between meeting rooms. The fledgling product team eventually took home the Web Award (in the Blog category) for that year. SXSW marks the moment of mass take-up for the tech community and Twitter's first moment of mass hype. *Gawker*'s Nick Douglas reported that Twitter had "blown up," with activity on the service jumping from 20,000 to 60,000 messages per day during the conference.[6]

The buzz reached us, too. We each created our own accounts in the first quarter of 2007. As people who study social life and the internet and who were already part of the blogging scene, Twitter had reached a level of importance that seemed to mandate our participation, or at least observation. Our own initial tweets reflect the site's allure, the aesthetic of the quotidian status update, and what was, at the time, a typical uncertainty about what Twitter was for. Jean's first tweet, posted from her original (and now private) account on 7 March 2007, was a direct and mundane response to the service's original prompt question, "What are you doing?":

> hunched over my computer as usual. But happy that it's raining outside!

Nancy's, posted a week later on 14 March, was even more typical of first tweets in the early years of the platform:

> Signing up for twitter even though I don't think I want it.

Like Jean's, Nancy's tweet followed the standard syntax of a personal update, with the addition of reflexive ambivalence about signing up to yet another social media service—a recognition that, back then, there seemed to be a new one launching just about every day. Gradually, alongside our friends, colleagues, and Twitter-only acquaintances, we experimented with different forms, genres, and purposes of tweeting, and took part in on-platform discussions and, sometimes, arguments, about the platform's emergent and competing norms.

Early on, there were debates about what using Twitter should even be called. In a sure sign that the service represented a new development in digital media, commentators experimented with various categories, with many calling it a "microblogging" service (as in Mark Glaser of *Mediashift's*[7] introductory Twitter and microblogging tutorial), some calling it a "social network" site, and others developing hybrid categories by virtue of comparison to existing services, like the then-popular MySpace or Dodgeball.[8] Jason Kottke's comparison of Blogger's and Twitter's early growth in the frequency of posts[9] demonstrates our habit of trying to make sense of new phenomena using existing categories, even when they don't quite fit. Twitter was not entirely unlike blogging, but it was definitely something distinct, something that didn't yet have a name, and yet something which seemed to threaten the blog platform business.

With a minimalist interface, guided only by a prompt that encouraged the expression of personal real-time experience in compact form, Twitter's ambiguity almost demanded that its users develop their own ideas about what to do with it. The earliest users, predominantly American technorati and bloggers—in other words, those already used to experimenting with and reflecting on their participation in new media—quickly developed and shared their ideas about how Twitter should be used. A form of public pedagogy emerged. Whether to help others out or gain attention as Twitter experts, bloggers wrote copious "what is Twitter, and how to use it" articles for at least the first few years of Twitter's existence.[10] Those posts that circulated on well-read blogs got the most attention. This meant that from the beginning, the public conversation about what Twitter was and what it should be used for was shaped significantly by tech influencers—mostly white, a lot of them men, and with technical expertise and professional identities tied up with journalism, software development, and especially blogging. A couple of years later, in the face of what seemed like a very deliberate attempt to shape Twitter's communicative norms in certain directions, and with the recent release of Jonathan Zittrain's book *The Future of the Internet—and How to Stop It*,[11] we began joking (on Twitter) about writing a book called *Twitter: You're Doing It Wrong—and How to Stop It*.

By mid-2007, the platform was receiving significant mainstream media and technology press attention. Politicians John Edward and Barack Obama were there by May 2007, as were leading international media outlets like the BBC, Al Jazeera, and the *New York Times*.[12] Meanwhile, a wide and diverse range of communities, subcultures, and scenes were finding Twitter and making it their own—comedians, fans of popular culture, academics, and activists. In the US, one of the earliest, most visible, and—because it made non-white cultural practices so obviously important—most attention gaining of these emergent communities was "Black Twitter," which André Brock describes as the use of Twitter's "rigid format to articulate Black discursive styles and cultural iconography [in a way that] subverts mainstream expectations of Twitter demographics, discourses, and utility."[13] In Australia, Indigenous cultural and intellectual leaders created innovative and culturally appropriate forms of media activism around the rotating @IndigenousX account (from which a different Aboriginal or Torres Strait Islander person tweets each week) and #IndigenousX hashtag, connecting Australia's Indigenous communities with each other and with First Nations people the world over.[14]

Attention from mainstream celebrities brought new users flooding to the platform. Oprah's first tweet, posted live on her show, was a major moment, not only for the platform's mass take-up, but for its presence as part of mainstream media culture. The event was beleaguered by technical difficulties and characterized by a touch-and-go atmosphere, feeding the mythology of the scrappy startup starting to make it big, while simultaneously revealing the company's less than robust technical systems and processes in these early years. The service was notorious for its unreliable infrastructure. The problems were so pervasive that when the site replaced its jokey "LOLcat" images with Australian artist Yiying Lu's illustration of a whale being lifted into the air by birds,[15] the image became so familiar to users that the expression "Fail Whale" came into stand in for Twitter's frequent outages, just as the "blue screen of death" came to stand in for crashes in the Windows computer operating system.

In these early years, Twitter reportedly went through stalled attempts to get acquired, involving talks and negotiations that came close to deals with Yahoo! in 2007 and Facebook in 2008, but with none of them coming to fruition, perhaps in part because of the difficulty the fledgling company had in articulating its purpose and vision. Twitter has an ongoing legacy of difficult relationships with other social media companies—impacting especially on the interoperability of Twitter with Facebook and Instagram. The service engaged in multiple experiments with possible business models (and multiple CEOs), coming to a head with its 2013 initial public offering of shares in the company to investors. Since going public, Twitter has retained a loyal core userbase and has grown steadily, particularly internationally, but it has consistently lacked the stratospheric year-on-year user growth demanded by investors and shareholders.[16]

The device and app ecosystem for Twitter has also changed very significantly over its lifetime. Like the technical side of @s, hashtags, and retweets, the apps we use to access Twitter have evolved, and their evolution has influenced how we experience, use, and think about the platform. There are two distinctive phases in Twitter's relationship with the third-party developer community. Initially, Twitter encouraged the development of apps that allowed people to access and use Twitter in different ways and on different devices, often delivering on ideas from the user community.[17] Around 2009, as Twitter matured and began to get serious about issues like the consistency of its visual branding, it began to exert more control over these third-party developments, through changes made to its application programming interfaces (APIs)—the coded instructions that tell one software application how to talk to another—and the developer rules associated with them. These changes significantly limited the entrepreneurial opportunities for third-party developers to build new businesses on the platform. A pattern began to emerge whereby Twitter bought up the third-party applications it wanted to incorporate into the platform, and locked the others out by changing the APIs and their rules.

These moves largely shut out third-party mobile app developers at the same time that users were migrating en masse to mobile devices. While user clients were the most visible face of this shutting out of third-party developers, it affected other services and tools originally developed outside the Twitter company itself. Examples include URL shortening services, image-sharing applications, and even search—the Twitter search function you use today was built on a third-party search engine developed by a company called Summize, which Twitter acquired in 2008.[18]

Indeed, the events of 2010 and 2011 emphatically mark Twitter's turn away from the Web 2.0 "open innovation" paradigm (within which value is added by third-party developers, and the return on investment for venture capitalists can be deferred at least for a while), toward a centralized, advertising-driven one, within which the user experience and user metrics need to be contained and controlled. And, as we have written about elsewhere, the restrictions on APIs—the key protocols that enable and constrain uses of Twitter's affordances and data by third parties—had a serious impact on data access for public researchers, too.[19]

Twitter's Competing Cultures

From the start, Twitter was an enigmatic platform—open to multiple uses, populated by passionate insiders, but mysterious to outsiders. As we will see, some common values have emerged among diverse stakeholders, such as protecting the integrity of the feed, the capacity to organize users and conversations, and giving appropriate credit to the ideas of others. Yet Twitter's meanings and role have always been ambiguous, and early usage patterns betray subtle but significantly different understandings of its purpose, the source of its potential value, and the kinds of relationships that were meant to be built and sustained between users. Amid all this diversity of uses, there has always been a particular tension between the idea of a simple social technology for updating your friends on the one hand, and an informational public communication platform on the other.

The original prompt for user updates (which could be performed via SMS or the website) focused clearly on real-time reporting of personal activity, asking "What's your status?,"[20] soon replaced with the more personal "What are you doing?," which remained in place for the first few years. The pitch to users was clearly focused on ambient intimacy[21]—the mundane sharing and peripheral awareness of everyday experiences, thoughts, and activities among small groups of close friends or colleagues.

From the beginning, the founders had dreams of the platform going global, but, as related by journalist Nick Bilton in his book *Hatching Twitter*, two of the main drivers of the platform in those first years, Jack Dorsey and Evan "Ev" Williams, had significantly different visions of the tool's purpose and value. According to Bilton, it was Ev who pushed for the 2009 change to the tagline from the status update question "What are you doing?" to the more news-oriented question "What's happening?"[22] in keeping with his insistence that Twitter was an information network rather than a social one. "Twitter is not a social network, it's an information network," Williams told a crowd at SXSW in 2009 (as Nancy, who was in attendance, noted that she was doing it wrong). The change was reported in a Twitter blog post (authored by Biz Stone), constructing a narrative of *progress* from a me-centered, personal, and intimate Twitter, to a world-centered, public, and newsy one:

> The fundamentally open model of Twitter created a new kind of information network and it has long outgrown the concept of personal status updates. Twitter helps you share and discover what's happening now among all the things, people, and events you care about. "What are you doing?" isn't the right question anymore—starting today, we've shortened it by two characters. Twitter now asks, "What's happening?"[23]

Twitter remains a site of uncertainty and contestation not only over what kind of communication it should be used for, but over the purpose and value of different kinds of human communication in general. Infamously, in the introductory post to marketing company Pear Analytics' widely reported content analysis of 2,000 tweets from the public timeline, Ryan Kelly wrote:

A while back we embarked on a study that evolved after a having a debate in the office as to how people are using and consuming Twitter. Some felt it was their source of news and articles, others felt it was just a bunch of self-promotion with very few folks actually paying attention. But mostly, many people still perceive Twitter as just mindless babble of people telling you what they are doing minute-by-minute; as if you care they are eating a sandwich at the moment.[24]

While forming part of ongoing debates about the relative social value of everyday or personal communication, the wide reporting of this story by leading news outlets including the BBC, CBC, and NBC, and the enthusiasm with which they picked up the factoid that 40% of tweets were "pointless babble," were also symptomatic of Twitter's media representation at the time.[25] In these first few years, Twitter was alternately hyped as the next new thing and dismissed as an oddity with at best marginal potential usefulness. As the media increasingly promoted Twitter's diffusion and cited its apparent role in events such as the 2009 Miracle on the Hudson and later the 2010–2011 series of popular uprisings in the MENA region known as the Arab Spring, the discourse legitimized Twitter as a global news source with a role to play in serious, newsworthy events. Even then, however, they probably could not have imagined an American president issuing commands to his nation's military via tweet.

Perhaps unsurprisingly, given that journalists tend to cover what they perceive as "newsworthy," very few mainstream

media discourses ever offered any serious positive evaluation of Twitter's function in everyday, interpersonal communication, self-representation, and sociability, despite robust research exploring these aspects of the platform[26] and despite the significance of the convergence between personal and public communication that is social media's basic founding principle and that constructs its "habitus."[27] The tensions that had been there since the beginning—between the mundane and the spectacular, the self and the world—had always helped produce Twitter's unique culture, where friendly chatter, food updates, and pet portraits mingled with election campaigns and world news events.[28] But the discourses of professionalization and newsworthiness, as well as the turn to metrics of attention and engagement associated with the media business, have tipped the balance, changing Twitter, including the company's own view of itself, in important ways. Pleasure and fun, once widespread, even defining qualities of the site, can now feel like acts of resistance.[29]

Studying Platforms

In order to understand these changes, and more broadly how the contemporary digital media environment works, we need a systematic framework for framing and analyzing its dominant platforms. It's tempting to view Twitter as a single "technology"—a static object that can be cast as a causal agent of societal change. A closer look reveals a more emergent, dynamic truth, one in which platform companies, their technologies, and their cultures of use co-evolve over time. To fully understand how these platforms change, we need a strategy that lets us observe these complex relationships and processes. Yet despite their ever-present accessibility, platforms and the companies that provide them are closed to public oversight, making it difficult for outsiders to study and report on them, and even harder to preserve their histories—an increasingly pressing problem for researchers and archivists.[30]

In this book, we introduce an original approach to this challenge: the platform biography. While we apply it to Twitter, the model can be used to study other platforms and apps as well. In an era of tightening access to platforms' data, the platform biography approach can be used and understood by researchers, students, and everyday users, without the need for privileged insider access to social media companies. Twitter's story is part of a bigger one: the story of how our media environment has changed over the past ten years—sometimes dramatically, sometimes gradually, but rarely undetectably.[31] In this book, we show how a multilayered approach centered on the changes in specific platform features can help us understand both changes in Twitter's culture and changes in how the internet is organized, and in whose interests, over time.

When we call Twitter a "platform" in this book, we mean far more than either the back-end technical architecture that supports social media services, or the companies that provide those services. Rather, we understand platforms like Twitter to be made by the relations among a number of elements:

- "Frontstage" user interface and features (the box that invites you to post an update, the layout you see and actions you

can take when you use the Facebook website, a Google map, or the Instagram app)

- "Backstage" software, algorithms, and APIs (the combination of data and algorithms that power Twitter's trending topics, the contents and ordering of an individual Facebook newsfeed, or suggestions of related YouTube videos to watch)
- The ecosystem of devices and services in which a platform is situated and connected (advertising networks, mobile phones and their operating systems and app stores, and the connections between your Spotify, Tinder, and Facebook accounts)
- Communicative or expressive content (Twitter jokes, YouTube videoblogs, or Instagram self-portraits, and the platform-specific ways these are shared)
- The practices and understandings of individuals and cohorts of users (including competing social norms about behavior or styles of communication, e.g., whether Twitter bots are a negative or benign presence on the platform; whether or not you should share your child's baby pictures on Facebook)
- The aims, interests, and business model of the organization that provides the platform (the operations, strategies, and financial aspects of Twitter, Inc., as distinct from Twitter as a user experience or a social space; the growth and profit-motivated decisions of Facebook as distinct from the inter-personal and group relationships maintained there)
- Public discourse about and media representations of the platform (e.g., news stories about the importance of Twitter in the Arab Spring, or the dangers of selfie culture on Instagram).

Previous studies of digital media platforms provide powerful approaches for getting at each of these aspects, but it is very hard to get them all together in one place.

In this book, we use interviews, tweets, media reports, and historical artifacts like blog posts and screenshots to paint a picture of the constant and ongoing struggles among a range of internal and external stakeholders over the purposes, meanings, and value of Twitter. In particular, we map struggles between competing cultures of use in which informal, interpersonal sociality butts up against a focus on information, newsiness, and professionalism. We highlight how features invented by users to address their problems are ultimately appropriated by the platform to generate metrics that favor commercial logics and open doors to antisocial uses and manipulative practices. Although we focus on Twitter, the content, practices, data, and business arrangements we describe in what follows flow across platforms and are shaped in relation to the broader digital media ecology.

In doing so, we are contributing to a growing subfield of scholarship. Since the mid-2010s, digital media scholars have begun to engage in earnest with the sociotechnical aspects of platforms, combining software studies (which attends to the material and code layer of communication technologies) with political and cultural economy to explicate platform features. For example, Hallinan and Striphas[32] undertook a detailed analysis of the Netflix content recommendation algorithms and their role in curating screen culture; Crawford and Gillespie[33] explored the material and ideological aspects of content flags—the mechanisms for making complaints to a platform provider about bad behavior—highlighting how despite engaging users more in content moderation, these mechanisms also constrain user agency significantly; Postigo[34] described how "technological features designed into YouTube" in service of the company's business interests—for example, metrics of audience engagement—also come to influence the kinds of uses that are valued and focused on by creators; while Bucher[35] analyzed how Facebook's EdgeRank algorithm works to argue it creates a "regime of visibility," which in turn results in a sensed "threat of invisibility" on our behalf as Facebook users, or "participatory subjects." This work has helped to advance the field, enabling us to understand more about how platforms do what they do and the influence they have on society and culture, by getting in close to the complexity of particular digital objects and devices.

In their study of YouTube, Burgess and Green[36] made an early attempt at the holistic study of a new digital media platform. They paid attention both to YouTube's structural affordances and its cultures of use, using the methods of the medium itself to examine the ways it was remediating popular culture and communication (by undertaking a content analysis of the most popular content as measured by the platform). But the book's first edition was a snapshot that didn't provide an account of change over time, and beyond these metrics of popularity, it didn't look in much detail at YouTube's technical affordances or underlying architectures in relation to its emerging and evolving business model. The second edition[37] goes some way toward engaging these topics, but the snapshot remains just that: the empirical work on how the platform constructs and reflects popular culture cannot be repeated because YouTube's architecture and affordances have changed fundamentally, so that the necessary data for comparison simply does not exist.

José van Dijck's treatise on the emergence of a "culture of connectivity" across some of the major web platforms, including YouTube, Twitter, Flickr, and Wikipedia, is among the more magisterial attempts to bring together the sociotechnical, cultural, and economic aspects of social media.[38] In her book, each platform is deployed discretely rather than comprehensively to discuss a particular aspect of the "culture of connectivity," an umbrella term for what van Dijck elsewhere describes as "social media logics."[39] Social media logics apply across a range of platforms and structure our contemporary media and communications environment more broadly. The idea is that the ways that social media are coming to influence our society, economy, and culture have antecedents in Altheide and Snow's concept of "media logic,"[40] in turn inspired in large part by the work of Raymond Williams on television.[41] Media logic is understood by van Dijck and Poell as "a set of principles or common sense rationality cultivated in and by media institutions that penetrates every public domain and dominates its organizing structures."[42]

Building on this model, van Dijck and Poell argue that social media has started to escape the bounds of its original institutional and everyday contexts and affect many other areas of life. Van Dijck and Poell propose that social media logic is spreading throughout society as social media become more ubiquitous and embedded in our lives beyond social networking and everyday status updates—impacting the mainstream media through news and journalism practices, and beyond them to politics and activism. They identify four grounding principles of social media logic: programmability, popularity, connectivity, and datafication. In Twitter's biography, we see how the platform has embedded and institutionalized these principles.

But while van Dijck and Poell do note the two-way character of programmability, where users have significant agency and input into content generation, curation, and popularity,[43] this theoretical model is still missing a sense of platforms' rich *cultures of use*—how they are given form and meaning through everyday life, and through the practices of diverse individuals, communities, and publics. Indeed, as our telling of Twitter's story argues, these principles became code in large part through haphazard, emergent, iterative processes in which the users were crucial actors.

The approach we take to how Twitter changed from an intimate messaging service to whatever it is now builds on this model: the platform (as a business and a technology) and its cultures of use shape each other over time. But actually observing this mutual shaping, either as it's happening, or afterward, is challenging. As LaFrance and Meyer write:

> Everything we know from experience about social publishing platforms—about *any* publishing platforms—is that they change. And it can be hard to track the interplay between design changes and behavioral ones. In other words, did Twitter change Twitter, or did we?[44]

As social media platforms like Facebook, YouTube, and Twitter have survived the decades, they have become attached to coming of age narratives. They have grown up, as the story often

goes, from rough-and-ready beginnings to become mature companies, transforming themselves from silly or trivial internet technologies to serious and important media platforms. Facebook's mantra of "move fast and break things" worked for its childhood, but when it turns out that democracy might be among the things it breaks, the mantra doesn't seem so great anymore.

In another example of this "growing up" narrative, Richard Rogers has described the process of Twitter's "debanalization" as an object of research, by which he means it has transformed from an apparently trivial website to a more mature news sharing platform, thus becoming a source of meaningful research data.[45] This framing of an early, everyday Twitter as "banal" (a pejorative term for the ordinary and everyday), later growing into a more newsy, and hence more significant, platform, is no accident. Society's most powerful institutions—like media organizations, academia, and technology companies—tend to value media and communication forms and practices that reinforce their own legitimacy. This means that they tend to frame political activism, science, and newsgathering as important and worthy uses of social media, while engagement with popular culture, everyday life, and personal relationships are framed as "banal" and even unhealthy.

Over time, the overvaluing of these kinds of public communication and the devaluing of everyday, personal ones have had a serious impact on Twitter's design and cultures of use. Our take on Twitter's "debanalization" is that the shift to an emphasis on news, information, and media over the emphasis on supporting the ambient intimacy of interpersonal connection opened the doors to the problems of Twitter's later years, including the bots, disinformation campaigns, and other appropriations of its affordances to influence nations and politics on scales it could never have comprehended in its infancy.

José van Dijck tells a different story, but it is an equally familiar one. In her account, Twitter's story is that of a fall from grace. Van Dijck describes Twitter's "interpretative flexibility" in its early years—a state where (almost) anything seemed possible, in which the potential uses, purposes, and configurations of Twitter were relatively open to experimentation and contestation.[46] But more broadly, she situates Twitter as a key player in a story of the corporate takeover and enclosure of the relatively open and participatory culture of the web. Many of the prototypical social media services built on the technical and ideological foundations of Web 2.0 in the early 2000s began as small-scale "indeterminate services for the exchange of communicative or creative content among friends," often without a clear market orientation.[47] With an explosion in scale over the next decade came the development of various competing business models and either acquisition by bigger players (like Google in YouTube's case; Yahoo! in Flickr's) or the conversion from start-up to major corporation (in the case of Facebook and Twitter), which absorbed the ideals of participatory culture into the logics of capitalism, commodifying our personal relationships in the process. This narrative is one of technical enclosure as much as it is one of market capture—social media platforms "epitomize the larger conversion from all-purpose devices to linear applied services,"[48] representing themselves as neutral "utilities" when they have actually "unquestionably altered the nature of private and public communication."[49] For van Dijck, only the resolutely not-for-profit Wikipedia stands outside this historical trajectory.[50]

The disheartening story of a journey that begins with discovery, exploration, and innovation and ends in enclosure and stagnation is common in critical discussions of the internet. It looks increasingly like the end of an earlier, more innocent era that was animated by ideas of participatory culture and user-led innovation, and a pivot toward the increased concentration of ownership and control typified by the turn to closed apps and mysterious algorithms. More than a decade ago, Jonathan Zittrain wrote with urgency about the corporate and technical enclosure of the internet, alarmed by the iPhone and its status as an unhackable, noncustomizable, "tethered appliance."[51] But, in a turn of events that might—or might not—offer a glimmer of hope, Zittrain could not have anticipated the explosion of third-party innovation that Apple's app store and later the Google Play store for Android afforded.[52]

The idea—implicit in popular and academic commentary alike—that profound changes in the media environment are inevitable and linear, leading only to the centralization of power and wealth in the hands of large platform companies, can leave us—as users, as citizens, as scholars—feeling powerless. Yet, as van Dijck notes, material changes to the technical and regulatory mechanisms of platforms, while they might not be noticed at the time, are *detectable*, even after the fact.[53] It should therefore be possible to diagnose such changes, observe the patterns in them across different platforms, and perhaps even identify opportunities for future intervention.

It is especially important here to notice the continuous updating of the core underlying technologies and affordances that constitute social media platforms, and that partly define their uses and meanings. These technologies are continuously being made and remade—and the modern software industry famously celebrates the idea that their artefacts never get finished at all. In fact, the idea of a continuously shipping product in "permanent beta"[54] whose improvements were fed by user contributions was a constitutive Web 2.0 ideology, one that has become embedded in the practices of app developers and publishers. The principles of permanent beta and continuous updating are hardwired into the operating systems of our smartphones, which, left to their default settings, will update themselves frequently, seemingly at random, and without requiring a specific decision on our part, but sometimes causing consternation, disruption, or frustration.

This continual making and remaking of apps, including social media platforms, is characterized by a process that Acker and Beaton refer to as "social churning."[55] While in certain circumscribed ways, social media platforms are actually co-created by users, they are also constantly and gradually changing at the hands of their designers, developers, and owners. Incremental changes have become so normalized for smartphone users that apps update themselves in the background without us noticing most of the time. But it is still the case that more visible, transformative updates create moments of acute discussion and contestation—forms of user dissatisfaction that Acker and Beaton refer to as "software update unrest."[56] In telling the stories of platforms, we might explore moments where such ritualistic modes of resistance might translate into opportunities for meaningful activism, diverting or arresting platform changes that are perceived to be detrimental to the cultural and social values users project onto and invest in them.

Writing the Platform Biography

Having discussed the "platform" part of the platform biography approach extensively, it is also worth saying a few words about our choice of the term "biography" to describe our process of studying and telling the story of how social media technologies, business models, and cultures of use co-evolve. After all, while it can certainly be scholarly, the biography is traditionally a literary form of life writing, rather than a scientific genre.

Translated literally from the Greek, the biography is a life record; it is also a literary genre. Though this book isn't very literary, "biography" is useful for us *because* of its literary genealogy. Even in cases where the subject's life is already a matter of public record (as in the case of media celebrities or famous politicians), any biography is inevitably partial, based on fragments of ephemera and interviews with unreliable bit players in the person's life, especially given that biographies are sometimes posthumous. Where they are written about living people, of course, they may be left behind by current events and therefore may need to be frequently revised and updated—and that is also very relevant here. Finally, just as no biographer, however intimately acquainted with their subject, can really offer unfettered access to the inner workings of the person whose life is being written about, neither can we usually get inside the companies that provide the platforms—at least not without a very privileged kind of access, one that is unavailable to most researchers and students. So, at a conceptual level, the platform biography approach provides the foundation for a dynamic empirical approach that generates a narrative of change by weaving together the stories of material objects, social relations, and events, and that therefore brings onto the stage the human lives that have intersected with and shaped the platform in question. After all, the life stories of social media platforms are our stories, too.

Thanks to past work in cultural studies and anthropology, the idea of the biography is already available for use in the study of material objects or technologies. As a form of life writing, the biography is inevitably and profoundly social, involving the subject's family origins, friendships, and relationships in specific historical contexts—and so it is with things as well, including technologies. In museology and cultural anthropology, scholars have written the social biographies of objects[57]—and here, the biography is concerned not just with what the form and function of a clay pot or a Bronze Age mirror can tell us about society at the time, but also the social history of the object itself—the hands it passed through, and the way it was designed, produced, and shaped by social relations. In contemporary culture, scholars have demonstrated how to approach everyday objects as if they have social lives. Appadurai's rich edited collection on the social life of commodities and consumer objects,[58] in fact, contained an article on "the cultural biography of things," in which Kopytoff discussed the social process by which things become commodities. The approach taken by Paul Du Gay and co-authors in their foundational work on cultural studies methods, [59] which exemplified the "circuit of culture" approach through the story of the Sony Walkman, was a powerful way of revealing how a consumer device can both carry with it and transform social relationships, and how these relationships have a life cycle. We believe that in the study of digital media technologies, which literally mediate social relations and which are constantly changing under the hands of so many different social actors, the "biography of things" approach works particularly well.

Writing a platform biography depends on collecting the appropriate materials. First, to map out the outlines of the platform's history, we gathered existing scholarly research on early Twitter's features and users.[60] We have made extensive use of tech-industry materials, third-party developers' blogs, and published company histories, drawing particularly on Nick Bilton's book *Hatching Twitter*,[61] online sources like *TechCrunch*'s company database Crunchbase, and hundreds of articles from business magazines and relevant sections of major newspapers. A crucial tool has been the Internet Archive's Wayback Machine[62] (especially for observing changes to the Twitter landing page, taglines, and user homepage, as well as user guides and terms of service). Some versions of the Twitter homepage and Twitter account pages at various points in the history of the platform have been archived, showing changes in the interface design, how different features were implemented and worked, as well as the syntax and style of tweeting during different periods of Twitter's history. We also draw on mainstream media coverage at key points, especially noting the adoption of Twitter as part of journalistic practice, discourses around its value as a platform for news and public communication, and the growing pressure on Twitter to grow exponentially once it became a public company.

Second, we drew on a wide range of background materials to tap most of the aspects of a platform we have identified in this introduction. An important set of sources was marketing blogs and tech blogs' how-to articles and reports on platform changes. Especially in the earlier years of Twitter, when social media existed alongside an active blogging culture, early adopters and lead users regularly wrote articles about feature and platform changes, providing detailed descriptions, critiques, and discussions of the implications of such changes for the future of the platform. But it is important to note here that the propensity to publish opinion pieces on the technical and social aspects of platforms has been unlikely to be widely shared across the demographics and cultures that constitute Twitter's userbase, even in those first few years. The coverage and discussion that we are drawing on is therefore skewed toward existing networks of mostly male tech bloggers, based in the US and other countries with high levels of English competence. At the same time, this skew reflects the outsized influence these voices have had. Twitter was founded in the US in English, and wasn't widely available in any other languages until 2010. Most of the extant material is tied to white elitist tech culture because they had an online presence, tech skills, and interest and ability to preserve the blogs that articulated their perspectives. But as other tech histories and analyses of other communities of Twitter users remind us, this is a very partial view, and creative, minority, and marginalized communities were doing plenty of innovative things with Twitter from the very beginning as well.

Third, the everyday practices and understandings of users are very significant in the generation, negotiation, and redefinition of the norms and conventions or "platform vernaculars" that make Twitter what it is.[63] This user perspective is embedded implicitly throughout our book. We have drawn on our own experiences and tweets and included examples of them here and there. We have mined our own tweet archives to help build the retrospective timeline of different features and how they were used. We bring in examples of tweets and posts in which users are reflexive and critical about platform affordances, cultures of use, and changes in their own public blog entries from the time.

To engage even more deeply with user perspectives, we interviewed a small number of regular users of the platform. These interviews were conducted in the United States in the spring of 2013. We recruited these participants through posts to Twitter and through the Social Media Collective blog at Microsoft Research. Since we were in the higher education–suffused locale of Cambridge, Massachusetts, at the time, the call attracted participants who were not only well educated but also unusually technologically literate. This was in some sense helpful, as they were able to articulate qualities of the platform and its norms that may have been harder for less savvy users to speak, and because even they, it turned out, saw their own practices as guided by so much more than the platform's changing interfaces and affordances. Other users we spoke with had very different levels of technical experience, and while some had been very early users with long, continuous careers on the platform, others had joined more recently.

We asked the interviewees to download their archives before the interview, to read through their tweets, and to identify points at which they felt that their tweeting practices had changed. During the interview, we projected their archives on a screen and let them walk us through their personal tweeting histories, beginning with their first tweet and going through the point where they felt their practices represented their current state. Explicitly engaging users (including ourselves!) in reflecting on their Twitter careers—effectively engaging them as oral history informants on the history of the platform—has helped us generate particular insights. The interviewees, too, expressed surprise at seeing their practices through this lens, rediscovering earlier practices and identifying changes in Twitter's cultures that had been forgotten or that had not been salient at the time.

In drawing on these found materials and reconstructed narratives, we make no claim to global population representativeness; indeed, quite the opposite. The blog entries and tech journalism pieces are remnants of the very particular public pedagogies and vernacular debates about Twitter's cultures of use that have contributed to shaping it all along the timeline. These public debates, as we discuss elsewhere, are undoubtedly weighted toward the interests and concerns of those who are most likely to have a public presence on tech interests in the first place. We offer the interviewees' stories not as generalizable to the whole of Twitter users, nor as exhaustive of the possibilities of Twitter use in the years they recount, but as indicative of the range of experiences users could have had.

Thankfully, Twitter has also been unusually transparent in preserving traces of its past. It appears that the official company blog was preserved in its entirety on the Twitter website, providing a rich source of information on changes to the platform's affordances and company discourse from its first days of existence on, as were various older versions of its official developer forums, FAQ, and user tutorial materials, which can be accessed via time-limited Google searches.

Finally, Twitter likes to tell its own life story. Media of all kinds love to memorialize themselves—anniversary specials have been a regular feature of television networks since their black-and-white days[64]—and social media companies are no exception. Twitter has authored its own hagiographies with great enthusiasm—examples include the country-specific series of blog posts and ancillary media around Twitter's 10th birthday.[65] The good thing for researchers is that they do this at regular intervals, so that the memorializations themselves become historical markers, despite the countervailing desire on behalf of the companies to focus on the present and the future. Each of these sources has value in isolation. Yet when we look at them together, we can see not just the changes in interfaces or business models, not just the changes in media coverage, not just the lives and social relationships of users, but the dynamic interplay of all of them, working together to incrementally shape Twitter's culture, and to recast its possible futures.

A Focus on Features

Many of Twitter's key features originated from emergent practices and shared conventions developed by the early user community. These usage conventions were unanticipated by or even ran counter to the expectations of the platform's founders, as they have at times readily and openly acknowledged. Some of these add-ons were later picked up by Twitter and turned into functioning features of the platform. Even the noun "tweet" to describe a post to the site and the verb "to tweet" to describe the act of posting such a contribution were user inventions. Both were initially resisted by the company, which preferred the more technical language of the "status update." Despite the term appearing in the names of numerous third-party applications like Tweetie and TweetDeck, Twitter did not apply to trademark "tweet" until 2009, and had to battle one such third-party service before eventually securing it in 2011.[66]

In the course of our interviews and archival research, it became evident that there was something especially important about three of the features for which Twitter is best known—the @, the hashtag, and the retweet, and the ways the practices and norms surrounding them had changed over time. Each was proposed by users in 2006 and 2007, when Twitter was still finding its feet. Initially user driven, they were incorporated by the platform in ways that ultimately came to drive the datafied, metricized, newsy, promotional platform we have now. These three features have become part of the grammar for understanding different uses of Twitter, including in academic research that employs the computational analysis of data gathered using the Twitter APIs to study the patterns of public communication enacted on the platform. Furthermore, their iconography—and, to an extent, their functionality—has become ingrained in social media logics across platforms.

In hindsight, this shouldn't have surprised us. The distinctive cultures of social media platforms owe much to the particularities of their user interfaces. Facebook's "like" button, newsfeed, and status update box; Tumblr's "reblog" button; and so on—each of these gives their host platforms some of their unique cultural flavor. But some platform features are actually the keys to participation on that platform as well, and so—as user-experience designers know—their form, format, and symbolic character matter enormously. Take, for example, the "new tweet" button in Twitter clients and the status update box with its empty space and its (once 140-, now 280-) character limit waiting to be filled with your answer to the question "What's happening?" Different ways of designing and framing this feature—like asking the question "What are you doing? [in your everyday life]" instead of "What's happening? [in the world]"—change the character of the uses to which we are invited to put them, subtly but fundamentally shifting the communicative purposes of the platform, at least in terms of how they are expressed to us.

Behind the scenes, such features (including both how they appear to users and how they work on the "back end") are also *protocological objects*[67]—through the exchange, ordering, and management of data, they mediate and set the terms of connections between users, content, and the company. They are agents of van Dijck and Poell's "social media logics,"[68] making cultural participation, human communication, and social connection calculable through processes of datafication. In short, key features provide the chief affordances of any particular platform; the flipside of this is that they are among the primary mechanisms of control as well.

As Taina Bucher,[69] drawing on Michael Serres,[70] notes, such features—understood as sociomaterial objects—are key mediators among the competing interests that produce Twitter as a platform and a cultural phenomenon, and they have an "enactive power" over the relationships between these actors (between users and the company; among the company, advertisers, and developers; and among users) and over the forms and formats of Twitter's content. Features are not passive objects through which human activities flow, but "active participants" and "protocols that structure and exercise control over the specific social situations on which they are brought to bear." At the same time, within the limits of technical possibility, users often resist, subvert, or creatively work around the intended uses of such features—they are rich sites of controversy that can reveal much about the politics of the relationships between users, technologies, and cultures of use. Studying the protocols—or features—of a particular platform is more manageable than trying to study the platform as a whole, but can be just as revealing of how it has changed over time.

In the following three chapters, we tell the stories of each of Twitter's three primary features. In order of historical incorporation by Twitter into its interface and algorithms, they are: the @ (created as a way to address and connect to other users); the # (a way to coordinate groups and topics); and the retweet (a way to share other users' contributions accurately and with attribution). The stories of these three features follow similar pathways, together showing how Twitter ended up where it was by the time we wrote this book, and hopefully offering clues to how it got to be whatever it is by the time you read it. We break this feature pathway into four stages—appropriation, incorporation, contestation, and iteration—and explore each feature using this scheme.

First, new conventions and practices are appropriated from other contexts and suggested by users in order to meet one or more needs that weren't served by Twitter's existing architecture or interface. These conventions and practices are taken up by other users, and also sometimes by third-party developers, who create new tools built on the Twitter platform to make these conventions available to more users—turning conventions into emergent features. Through this process, different models of how to use the features emerge and struggles over the "right" way to use them become common. Second, Twitter incorporates the feature into the platform's interface and algorithms. In doing so, they acknowledge the needs the users sought to fulfill with the feature while serving their emerging business model, seeking to make Twitter more seamless for new users, in pursuit of growth, and more datafied, in pursuit of opportunities to monetize that growth. The Twitter platform's incorporation of these new features solves some problems, but creates others. In the third phase, contestation continues. As our research shows, there was much more variety in how people used the @ or the retweet convention before official "support" hardwired these practices as features and in doing so stabilized their uses and meanings. But even after this apparent "hardwiring," users continue to reshape the meanings of Twitter's features. In the fourth stage, Twitter iterates their now officially adopted and embedded features, modifying how they look and work in the interface or the algorithmic back end. These further changes prove to be controversial among users, helping us to understand the ongoing, evolving struggles over Twitter's culture and social purpose.

1 The @

The "@" feature is the key to Twitter's role as a medium for conversation, and is essential for creating, maintaining, and enlivening connections among users. In a platform designed to announce rather than converse, it is emblematic of users' insistence on their capacity to reorganize in order to socialize. Invented by users very early on in the life of the platform, the @ has been continuously modified, resisted, and redefined by both users and the company in the years since.

In an article on user-led innovation in the *New York Times*, co-founder Evan Williams was quoted in 2009 saying that the @ symbol—one of the first community-invented usage conventions, used to mention or reply to other users—"really took [them] by surprise." He enthused about this innovation from the periphery, saying that "Twitter struck an interesting balance of flexibility and malleability that allowed users to invent uses for it that weren't anticipated."[1] The story of the chang-

  ⊕   The @

ing uses and affordances of the "@" is central to understanding how Twitter has mediated conversation and discussion among users over time.

Appropriation

Twitter initially launched as a service for narrowcasting personal updates to your friends, primarily via mobile phone. At the time, its prompt asked users to respond to the question "What are you doing?" Given this purpose, at small scale it needed very few features—you followed the updates of your friends, selectively receiving them via text message, and broadcast your own in return. If you wanted to know what was going on in the world (at least the world of early users), you could check the public timeline where all tweets from public accounts were streamed in a single, real-time feed. For users in the United States, given the pricing models for text messages on most US mobile phone carriers at the time, Twitter offered a lower-cost (in both effort and money) means for people to update each another. The integration of Twitter into mobile phones from the start was part of a burgeoning of new platforms that took advantage of mobile media to integrate location information into social networking. For example, the Dodgeball and Foursquare apps were both developed to help people let one another know their locations. While Twitter was not originally designed as a locative media technology, the earliest uses of the @ symbol, in tweets posted by Twitter's founders, echoed its use on Dodgeball, marking location or activity (literally signifying where a user was "at"). In response to the query "What are you doing?" a user might say they were "@work" (at work) or "@thebeach" (at the beach).

These uses emerged very early. On 22 March 2006, Odeo employee (and one of the engineers who created Twitter in a hackathon at the company) Dom Sagolla (@dom) posted a status update to let his friends know he was out and about doing errands. The tweet, which was the first to contain the @, reads simply, "@errand."[2] In a blog post, Sagolla recalls that this was a practice he had imported from Internet Relay Chat (IRC).[3] A few days later, on 24 March, Ev Williams (@ev) marked his breakfast location by tweeting "breakfst burrito @ herbivore. Mm!"[4] and, on 28 March, Jack Dorsey (@jack) used the full spelling "at" to accomplish a similar objective, tweeting "at work."[5] That three of Twitter's earliest employees used @, or "at," to indicate status or location rather than to address other users is indicative of the tensions between their original visions for Twitter and the new practices that the larger community of early adopters would soon invent and spread.

Tied so closely to mobile phone use and existing friend networks, connections between users were wired into the interface only at the level of friends (followees) and followers. As the site grew, more users accessed it through the website, and conversation networks expanded. People found themselves struggling to indicate that a message was responding to someone else, to point to other users, and to make connections visible within conversations. Addressing every tweet to what was starting to feel like the whole world wasn't working. They turned to the @.

In doing so, Twitter users were appropriating a symbol that already had a long history of being used to organize online interaction. First developed in typography and shorthand as a means of indicating "at" (as in "5 barrels of wine @ fifty dollars a barrel"), it became part of the internet's core architecture when it was appropriated to specify the server locations of email accounts. This gave the @ symbol both locative and communicative properties, specifying where a message should go, and also for whom it was meant. Developed not long after email, IRC also used the @user convention, as did many online environments of the 1980s and early 1990s, such as MUDs and MOOs.

While there have been competing claims to the invention of the @ convention, according to a blog entry by Twitter user and sleuth Garrett Murray,[6] the first use of @ user syntax to address another user on Twitter appears to be this, from 3 November 2006 (note the use of "twittering" instead of "tweeting"):

> @ buzz—you broke your thumb and youre stlll lwittering?
> that's some serious devotion—Robert Andersen @rsa[7]

In several other examples from around the same time as this blog post, and in fact involving the same network or community of users, we see the same space between the @ and the username. This use of the @ symbol preceding another user's name started to become a regular convention for addressing other users, and from November 2006 some began publicly discussing this new convention, spreading the idea to additional users as they did. As Honeycutt and Herring observed in one of the first empirical studies of communication on the platform, by appropriating the @username convention for this purpose, users were instigating and insisting on a kind of networked conversationality that went against the grain of the original intentions of the designers, who saw Twitter as a mechanism for providing atomistic status updates rather than for discussion and ongoing interaction.[8]

Former Odeo developer and very early Twitter user Evan (aka Rabble) Henshaw-Plath dug further into the data to find the origins of the @. In a (now deleted) 2012 blog post, he reported that the first use of the syntax "@username," without a space between the @ and the name, to refer to or address another user was a conversation between developers Ben Darlow (@kapowaz) and Neil Crosby (@NeilCrosby) about how to develop a syntax for exactly this purpose. This extremely meta exchange, which occurred on 23 November 2006, went as follows:

> Ben Darlow @kapowaz
>
> wondering if there should be a pseudo-syntax for letting a Follower on twitter know you're directing a comment at them.

> Neil Crosby @NeilCrosby
>
> @kapowaz: probably

The two users then began a conversation about the syntax and how it might work technically.

A few months later, and apparently independently of this, other, less prominent users began addressing tweets to each other using the slightly different syntax "@ username/Real Name," with a space after the @ and no real consistency applied to the format of the username. Evidence from online discussions about the origin of the @ convention as well as our own personal archives suggests that there were (at least) three competing conventions—"@ username" with a space, "@username" with no space, and "@ Firstname Lastname." At this very early stage, there were no hyperlinks within tweets, and no aggregation or representation of @s within the platform. But even early on, the @ sign had multiple meanings, each creating a different form of address. It might have appeared at the beginning of a tweet to directly address a user, as in "@nancybaym are you going to the beach this afternoon?"; at the beginning of a tweet to reply to another user, as in "@jeanburgess, yep, see you there!"; or at the beginning of a tweet to refer to another user, as in "@nancybaym is going to the beach, so I'm going too." It could also be used in the body of a tweet to refer to (@mention) another user, as in "I'm going to the beach with @nancybaym."

Incorporation

In early 2007, only months after its emergence as a user convention, Twitter incorporated the @user (without a space between the @ and the username) syntax into the platform's architecture, so that the text "@username" became hyperlinked within the body of a tweet to the @-mentioned user's profile page on the Twitter website.[9] Prior to this, the only way of observing connections between users was to check whether or not they followed each other. The @username syntax enabled people to respond to, address, or mention users even if they weren't following each other. In a boon to Twitter's emerging business model, this added an entirely new, trackable, and potentially monetizable layer to the network architecture (or "social graph") of the platform.

Once embedded, Twitter continued to build on the @'s possibilities. In May 2007, the platform began aggregating each user's

accumulated replies and mentions and developed a corresponding page on the website (originally but no longer at https://twitter.com/replies), or a tab in third-party apps, where a user could see all the replies and mentions they had recently received.[10] With later redesigns came the Notifications tab, which collated all metrics of attention, including @replies or @mentions, retweets, and favorites (or likes); and as of early 2019 separated "@mentions" out from likes and retweets. The aggregation, and counting, of these markers of conversationality created a new set of metrics, and with that a new set of aspirations and exploits that continue to reshape the platform.

The integration of @ into Twitter's appearance and functionality encouraged conversationality and reshaped user practice. Daniel, one of our interviewees, was surprised on reviewing his Twitter archive to see how his own practices shifted as the @ reply became formalized in this way. Early on, his tweets were what he described as "the equivalent of a Foursquare status like, 'I'm here now,' or 'I'm doing this,' or 'This thing just happened to me,' or whatever." After the incorporation of @ into the platform however, he described his feed as "probably at least 50 percent conversation at all times, just @replies to people." In the interviews, though, users did not necessarily view such changes in their own practices as consequences of the changing functionality of the interface and underlying code. Daniel, for instance, attributed the shift in his practices to having more potential conversational partners available on Twitter. One user surmised in our interview that they must have started posting pictures to Twitter when they saw their friends doing it, but their tweet archives revealed that this change in their communicative practice had actually coincided with a change in the app they were using to post—possibly indicating they had acquired a smartphone for the first time.

Others did see their increased conversationality as tied to the feature's structural incorporation. Bob, one of our more technically minded interviewees, noted that the new "software helps you a little bit better by having those conversation threads." Yet even for such users, the transition to interface-driven @ replying was far from smooth. Bob bemoaned the system's limitations in managing long multiparty conversations. His circles began passing around jokes about this problem in the form of tweets "where it's like everybody's @s and then one word at the end." His strategy to work around this problem, replying directly to the first person in the thread, also failed "because we've broken the thread and we're like, 'Oh my God, why are we using this to talk anyway?'"

The @'s adaption after embedding was further fostered and complicated by Twitter's early decision to encourage open innovation through its APIs. Many users accessed Twitter through one of the many third-party clients developed using these APIs, each of which integrated the @ in different ways and afforded different communicative possibilities. Bob used multiple clients, and described the resulting challenges:

> With the other clients you can choose reply all or just reply original. And I also use HootSuite to do automated tweeting both on my account but on others, mainly for promotional stuff. And that has—I can click on the thing and see the conversation threaded within it but it doesn't

actually get the entire conversation. I'm realizing a lot of
clients have that same problem. They'll show you parts
of it but not all of it. And it's all there but it's not easily
accessible.

Once embedded in the infrastructures for reading and creating tweets, people began using the @ to accomplish personal
goals in their particular life circumstances. Consider, for instance, Nick, one of our interviewees. In the summer of 2010, he
did very little tweeting, and when he did, it was to keep in touch
with his best friend and other friends who were no longer in the
same town. When, some time later, he changed life course and
enrolled in a graduate program, he shifted from using the @ for
personal relationship maintenance to using its affordances of
addressivity, brevity, and asynchronous temporality for professional networking:

I started doing a lot of @ replies to my classmates, and
that's something you'll see through the beginning of fall
2011 through now, is a lot of @ replies, because that's
kind of something you ca—maybe you can't G Chat while
you're cramming all night but you can send someone a
tweet and you know they'll get it, and it's short and easy
to look at.

His contrast between the @ on Twitter and Google Chat ("G
Chat") is important. These features, indeed even Twitter, are
understood not in isolation, but in terms of what they afford
that other alternatives do not.[11]

Another interviewee, Fiona, likewise described her use of the feature as driven by her social circumstances. In one phase of her Twitter life, she had a friend she "was getting into long conversations with all summer and into fall," but when that friend stopped appearing on Twitter, her use of the feature dropped. Similarly, when she was living in another city and broke up with her boyfriend, she found herself alienated from their shared friendship circle on her primary (though not only) Twitter account:

> it definitely became less interactive, and I think I sort of didn't even really notice as much or care as much, because I was so busy interacting on my public account that I was getting my social connection through Twitter, and I was getting it with people that I connected with better.

The process of going through her archive in preparation for our interview made her realize how her @ practices corresponded to her romantic cycles:

> You can see my patterns of whether I'm talking back, like how many @replies versus just random internal monologue, random stuff on my personal account. All the drops correlate with breaking up with people.

While these examples show people using @s to converse with people they already knew, or to build relationships with those they had just met, as the feature proliferated, increasingly people found themselves interacting with strangers. The topics

that stimulated such interactions could be quite random. One woman we spoke with drew attention to the first of her tweets to receive a reply from a stranger. The topic? Her bewilderment at having seen someone with individual-toed shoes wearing socks. Some who were using the site professionally, such as Sonya, a journalist who posted links to her articles, began to feel a sense of obligation to respond when her readers used the @ feature to reach out to her directly. She describes the first time she interacted with a stranger on Twitter:

> This was a story I was being asked about and I'm replying to them, a random person. I didn't know this person. I think [it was] my first significant interaction with a random person that I felt like I had to engage with in a serious manner.

Sonya, who understood herself as someone "who doesn't talk to people much," was surprised to see how often she actually used the @ to talk with others in her Twitter archive. "Maybe I do, it turns out that I do, but in my head I'm not talking to people as much as just posting things that other people would find interesting to read."

Contestation

The conflicts between Twitter as a space for interpersonal connection and as a site for information exchange became clear from the @'s first uses as a reply function, as it gave form to Twitter's subversive conversationality. It didn't take long for there to be a backlash. When the @ was first integrated into the platform's

design, everyone who followed you could see every tweet you posted, including @reply conversations. Even before the feature was incorporated, users, finding their timelines filled with @ replies to strangers, took to the site to tell other users that they were using Twitter wrong or, as in the exchange below from 13 January 2007,[12] to defend the emerging uses of the @ from such critiques:

> **Nick Douglas @toomuchnick**
> My god, people! "@Bob" doesn't send just to Bob. Only send "@" messages if we will ALL care about them. GAAA AAAAAAAAAAAAAAAAAAAAAAAAAAAAAAAAAAAAAAAAAAH.

> **Kevin Marks @kevinmarks**
> @nick the point of using @ is to cue the rest of us in, and help us see why we might find nick amusing; we know how to use D.[13]

These early tweets go to the heart of what remains a core problem both for Twitter as a business and for users: any individual's feed contains a lot of content they don't care about and even actively wish to avoid. At the same time, some users value the ambient intimacy[14] with friends of friends, and pointers to interesting new people, that the visibility of others' @replies afforded. The struggle to protect the integrity of the feeds of one's own and others plays out in the face of countless ideas of what constitutes a tweet worth posting.

The @ can run afoul of users' concern with respecting others' streams. The growth of the Twitter user community, and the

growing dominance of representational frames that defined it as a news medium rather than a social networking site like the rapidly expanding competitor Facebook, meant that some users perceived this awareness of others' conversations as "noise." In fact, many people complained that, as it scaled up, the medium was becoming *too* conversational, implying that news and information should be separated out from the interpersonal communication of others,[15] as the following quote from a blog post by Eric Meyer shows:

> . . . the way people are using Twitter right now, it's rapidly becoming the most inefficient and unusable version of IRC ever. Look, people, if you want to chat, then get a chat room. You know?[16]

Users responded to what they perceived as the flood of irrelevant @s in their stream in diverse ways. One person we interviewed began using it as a mechanism to decide who and who not to follow. She described what happens when she looks at a user's profile for the first time:

> If I see all @replies, that makes me less interested in following them just because I know that the stuff that shows up in their stream is gonna be hard to follow. But if it's a celebrity or if it's somebody that I actually have an interest in following, I'll be more—like, I'll let it slide more often. But there have been certain people that I've been like, "Oh, I should follow so-and-so." And then I've been like, "Ooooh. All @replies. Never mind."

Her reluctance to follow conversational users stemmed from the apparent pointlessness of seeing only half a conversation, but also the fact that it became "a lot more work to follow the thread, because you have to click on it."

Michelle, an interviewee who worked in the tech sector but maintained relationships on Twitter with various circles of friends outside that world, responded to the problem by creating separate professional and personal accounts, the latter to track her friends and the former to follow the conversations in the tech industry that otherwise drowned out her friends. Daniel didn't think all this @ing was inherently problematic, but found it very annoying when:

> I say something and then someone replies to me and then someone replies to them and then they keep having a conversation with each other but they keep sort of cc'ing me on—but it's just like email in that case. It's like, "Please remove me from the cc." It's like please drop me from this Twitter conversation because you're filling up my @reply and I'm getting things on my phone.

Again, note the use of "email" and "the cc," earlier modes of online communication about which norms of appropriate usage had already developed.

Those who liked the visibility of @s to people they did not follow appreciated both the tips toward new people the feature offered and the general increased conversationality of Twitter. Eavesdropping has its appeals. "I think it's kind of interesting looking at other people's conversations," one interviewee told us.

Similarly, Anne described "a couple of people that I follow that have communications with each other. And so that's sometimes interesting, where I'm like, 'Oh, @reply to someone else I know. Let me click on this conversation and read it.'"

Another emergent set of concerns that emerged after the @ was incorporated into the platform centered on how it made interactions between people into performances of social connection in ways that could irritate both observers and those immediately involved. Daniel, for example, complained about couples using the @reply for "lovey-dovey stuff" when they "could DM each other or use text messaging or something and I don't really want to see this." "I think it's weird when people do stuff with @replies that I think should be done over DM," he continued:

> So for example, if you're just setting up a time to meet someone somewhere, like if I know two people and they're having a conversation like, "Oh, I'll meet you at four o'clock at wherever," I understand some of that's performative and you want to know that you guys actually have friends and some of that's like and maybe you're hoping that I'll join in and be like, "Hey, you're meeting at four o'clock at this restaurant. Great, can I join in?"

Michelle developed a large following early in Twitter's history. She was initially enthusiastic about the @reply until she "realized how performative it got" and was unable to deal with the scale. Flooded with messages directed at her, she found herself replying "to maybe probably one out of every 25 messages." She began switching media: "I'll see something that I want to reply to and I'll just drop an email. Because as I say I don't want the conversation to be performed like that." Even though it intensified the platform's conversationality, Michelle associated the increased use of the @ with a shift toward Twitter becoming "this thing that you did professionally. I associate it with a world of social media consultants, a world of how to be a good Twitter user, a world of having to be accountable for my poly-presence in ways that tend to annoy the hell out of me." She expressed sadness that she felt unable, as a visible personality on the site, to "actually engage people." For her, the feature's affordance of direct addressivity took away its fun.

Iteration

In early 2008, Twitter, responding to the challenges we've identified above, changed its defaults so that you could no longer see @replies directed at those you did not follow without choosing to do so by deliberately changing your settings, and in 2009 it removed that option entirely. While there was always a difference between @reply and @mentions, the changes to the @ reply function changed the actual format and function of tweets beginning with an @reply. Putting @ at the beginning of a tweet would make it behave differently, now excluding much of its previous audience. Including an @mention in the body of the tweet would simply create a hardwired reference to the person being mentioned.

Twitter first reported this as a "minor change" affecting only the 3% of users who had visible @replies switched on in their settings.[17] But it resulted in user outrage: Twitter "[burst] into flames"[18] and the trending hashtag #fixreplies emerged to co-ordinate protest and make it visible.[19] This hashtag was the top trending topic for at least a little while in the following days. Mashable writer Ben Parr summed up the change and why it had led to an "uproar":

> Here's what's happened: until today, you had three options for handling how you viewed @replied [sic]. You could show @replies from nobody, @replies from everybody, or only the @replies of people you were following, whether it was to them or from them. With the new update, there's only the last option available.
>
> The intent of the change seems to revolve around simplifying and reducing the noise of the Twitter stream for newer users. Yet the result also takes away a valuable way to discover new people, new conversations, and takes away options users previously had.[20]

Co-founder Biz Stone responded on the official Twitter blog with a post entitled "The Replies Kerfuffle,"[21] explaining the technical and product design reasons behind the change and acknowledging the poor communication that had accompanied its implementation. Stone repeated the argument that only "3%" of users wanted to see replies from users they followed to users they didn't, and that allowing this option was overburdening the system. It was a classic example of the company's perception that early adopters wanted Twitter to work one way while the masses that Twitter was trying to attract wanted something completely different: that is, that new users

The @

wanted simplicity and seamless usability, not the power to change every setting themselves.

Later, the act of responding to a tweet by clicking on the "reply" button would record the responses as a thread and display them that way in official clients, even if the @reply text was removed from the beginning of the tweet. This is an example of Twitter backgrounding functions, separating them from their textual representations within tweets themselves, as part of a more "seamless" user experience. As Stone's "Replies Kerfuffle" blog post demonstrates, the drive to create a seamless user experience is part of a quest to enroll new users who haven't already incorporated a particular technology's design quirks and conventions into the practice of everyday life—conventions that can seem obscure and difficult to negotiate for new users, a problem for which Twitter is infamous.

What seemed to be an elegant solution (who doesn't want seamless usability?) instead created new seams, glitches, and conflicts. Some users felt that at least some of the responses they wrote to others would be interesting to a broader readership than those who followed both parties. Others didn't realize there had been a change, and began tweets with @, unaware that such tweets would be seen only by users who followed both them *and* the person being addressed. This latter problem occurred most often when the @ was meant as a mention rather than a means of address. For instance, Nancy may have seen Jean presenting a paper and tweeted something like "@jeanburgess talking about the Australian Twittersphere," assuming her own followers who did not follow Jean would nonetheless see it.

In response to these problems, users who had become accustomed to the earlier conventions created a workaround to preserve public conversation, by putting a period (or full stop) before the @reply (as in ".@user"), returning the ability to make replies visible to one's own followers who didn't happen to follow the person one was replying to or mentioning. The hypothetical tweet above might then read ".@jeanburgess talking about the Australian Twittersphere." This solved the problem for users in the know, but the appearance of the period mark, let alone the nuances of how and when to use it for what purposes, added a new layer of confusion to the @ system just as Twitter was trying to make this very feature less confusing for newer or casual users. The in-group of highly active and influential Twitter users who understood the site's features and functions and knew how to manipulate them to meet their own needs and beliefs about how the platform should function grew further apart from the infrequent and new users the company wanted to woo, but who found the site a hodgepodge of impenetrable punctuation marks and disconnected thought fragments.

In the most distinctive manifestation of the trend toward seamless usability to date, in May 2016, Twitter announced to developers that the @ feature was going to go through an even more dramatic change:

> Goodbye, .@: These changes will help simplify the rules around Tweets that start with a username. New Tweets that begin with a username will reach all your followers. (That means you'll no longer have to use the ".@" convention, which people currently use to broadcast

Tweets broadly.) If you want a reply to be seen by all your followers, you will be able to Retweet it to signal that you intend for it to be viewed more broadly.[22]

This announcement came as part of a larger one in which Twitter notified the user and developer community about yet another significant platform redesign. Rather than radically expanding the allowable number of actual characters in each tweet, the virtual limit on characters was being expanded by allowing images and other media to be embedded without counting toward the character limit. The joke about long conversations ending in a tweet made only of @replies with no room left for content lost its punchline—Twitter was too neat and tidy for that now . . . at least on the surface.

2 The

Perhaps no single character has been as iconic a symbol of Twitter as the now-ubiquitous hashtag. The syntax of the hashtag has a few simple rules: it consists of the hash symbol (#) immediately followed by a string of alphanumeric characters, with no spaces or punctuation. It is used routinely in social media communication across a number of platforms including Tumblr, Instagram, and even Facebook, but its most important point of emergence and popularization was in Twitter. It is in Twitter that it remains the most comfortable fit, and it was Twitter that turned it into a highly significant, multifunctional feature. The hashtag has made its way off the internet, appearing regularly on television, in advertising, on products, and on protest signs around the world. From its beginnings as a geeky tool designed to help individual users deal with an increasingly fragmented information stream, Twitter has made the hashtag a new and powerful part of the world's cultural, social, and political vocabulary. The @ feature we have just discussed helped people organize into pairs and create conversational streams. The hashtag, which organizes tweets into topics, publics, and communities, goes to the heart of a crucial question: How is the internet organized and for whom?

Appropriation

Although its use on Twitter was new, the # has a prehistory both as a punctuation mark and as part of internet communication. Imported from elsewhere, as was the @, the hashtag brought some of its prior conventional understandings with it. Known as the "octothorpe" by typography experts, in early computer-mediated communication the hash or pound symbol was used to mark channels and roles in systems like Internet Relay Chat (IRC). It therefore worked to both categorize topics and group users.

The # was also closely tied to the crowdsourced content tagging systems common to the web era. On the music-streaming site Last.fm, for example, users could tag artists and songs, information the site used to "learn" about music and fuel recommendations and radio streams, laying groundwork for Spotify and other apps' current recommendation algorithms. User-contributed tags were an important affordance of the Flickr photosharing website, where they helped direct people to images and to one another—a practice that was carried over to Instagram.[1] Crucially, users could add as many tags to their Flickr photographs as they liked, creating a system that was less a taxonomy (an expertly ordered system based on exclusive, hierarchical categories) and more a "folksonomy" (a crowd-sourced one based on inclusive tags and aggregation). Folksonomical ordering, in the mid-2000s, was widely imagined as a more efficient, organic way of ordering content than categories or directories, and it was this model that underpinned the popular social bookmarking service del.icio.us.[2]

The Flickr folksonomy of user-contributed tags was paradigmatic of the Web 2.0 ideology—marked by a shift from the idea that web development was about serving content to *audiences* to one where the goal was building architectures of participation for *users* (sometimes distinguished from passive website "visitors") and the expectation that the user community's activities would add value to further applications built on these architectures. Reddit's systems for upvoting user-curated content in particular subreddits and modern Twitter's aggregated trending topics are contemporary versions of this early tag-based co-curation model.

As far as we know based on extant materials, the hashtag's use in Twitter was first proposed in mid-2007 by Chris Messina in a series of blog posts.[3] In Messina's view, the hashtag was a solution to a need. Remember that, at this time, it was still possible to see a public feed of every single tweet from a public account. Topical conversations among people who did not follow one another were incoherent at best. Given its technical character, it was clear that the users advocating for the hashtag were technically proficient (many of them also developers) with an active online presence, who positioned themselves as participants in a community of lead users. While some users were experimenting at this stage with hashtags, the idea was not taken up much until a particularly acute and sufficiently significant event—the

San Diego brushfires. In conjunction with this event, Messina achieved wider take-up of the hashtag as a tool for coordinating crisis communication by actively lobbying other lead users and media organizations.[4]

Although this rapidly unfolding disaster demonstrated a clear and legitimating use case, the broader meaning of the hashtag and its possible uses remained ambiguous. Despite this, Messina, as a tech-industry insider and lead user, continued to widely advocate for its use—even reportedly pitching it to the Twitter leadership. Nick Bilton relates an encounter between the Twitter founders and Messina at the Twitter offices as follows:

> "I really think you should do something with hashtags on Twitter," Chris told them. "Hashtags are for nerds," Biz replied. Ev added that they were "too harsh and no one is ever going to understand them."[5]

Recall that Twitter had recently begun wrestling with the problem (a problem that still haunts it) of conflict between the cultures of expert users that made the platform work for them and the new users they alienated but whom the company badly needed to sustain its growth. As this chapter will show, the hashtag provoked contestation between Twitter's different cultures of use in other ways as it was taken up both for the serious uses such as disaster and professional discussion Messina had envisioned and to create sociable rituals and play.

From the beginning, there was thus contestation around the right way to use hashtags. As Messina's own historical documentation and that of others show, there were several competing models of how and why to coordinate Twitter activity as the flow of tweets started to grow beyond an easily manageable size.[6] Perhaps the # was a tag, designed to help organize collections of tweets on shared topics? Or was it a way to form channels, or groups of *users* interested in those *topics*? Underlying these different models of what the hashtag could become were different models of Twitter: as an information network, a social networking site or online community, or a platform for discussion and the emergence of publics. Such ideas were still new and hotly contested at the time. Though the informational seems to have won out over the conversational model of Twitter, the hashtag remains, and is used for an astonishing array of social, cultural, and political purposes—some of them vitally useful, not all of them serious, and some of them downright toxic.

Over time, the practice of including hashtags in tweets was widely adopted by user communities. We have seen that the story of Twitter cannot be understood without looking at how third-party platforms and websites can shape practices on Twitter and help to influence or disrupt the platform's affordances. This is particularly evident with hashtags as, long before they were incorporated by Twitter into trending algorithms and search, third-party websites were developed to index and catalogue them. This enabled users to find and join conversations of interest to them—a project that was possible only because of Twitter's relatively small scale in its early years. For example, the website Hashtags.org was launched in December 2007, and provided a real-time tracking and indexing of hashtags before Twitter implemented search. Participants at an event, for instance, could visit the website to see other tweets from the same event.

The hashtags in the earliest archived version of the Hashtags. org homepage, from April 2008,[7] include a number of academic and tech conferences (#EconSM, #netco8, #interact2008), sporting and entertainment events (#idol, #yankees, #RED-SOX), and tweet categories (#haiku), and several examples of the use of hashtags for coordinating discussion topics and finding like-minded users (e.g., #seriousgames, #punknews, #college, #PHX), brands and products (#gmail, #firefox), and even people (such as *Wired* journalist #ChrisAnderson). The most tweeted hashtags are represented as amassing tweets numbering in the tens or at most hundreds, a reminder of the modest scale of Twitter at the time. Many of the later uses of hashtags, such as for humor, activism, or second-screen television viewing, had yet to emerge.

Incorporation

Ever since those early debates about whether Twitter needed "channels" (of topics) or "groups" (of users), hashtags have continued to play both structural and semantic roles: that is, they coordinate both communities and topics, helping users find each other and encounter a range of contributions to the discussion of issues and events. In July 2008, Twitter bought the startup Summize (which offered a search engine and basic analytics for tweets), hiring some of its engineers in the process, and then integrated Summize's core functionality into the Twitter platform as search.twitter.com. This added functionality enabled the Twitter platform to integrate hashtags by hyperlinking them to the search results for all tweets containing a given hashtag.[8] Hashtags also began figuring in the new feature of

The #

trending topics that Twitter was also working on in 2009. This period of early innovation (2007–2009) was followed by far more rapid growth in the Twitter userbase from 2010 onward. Since then, the hashtag has been widely and diversely applied, and has become embedded into the institutional logics of mainstream media companies, brands, and presidential campaigns, as well as being applied to platform-specific forms of poetry and humor and the coordination of "ad hoc publics" concerned with both formal and informal political issues.[9] Hashtag studies has become an entire subfield of social media research because of the way that hashtags organize data on particular topics of relevance to particular communities—see, for example, Nathan Rambukkana's edited collection on the subject, *Hashtag Publics*.[10]

The hashtag has fostered the rise of Twitter as a platform for news, information, and professional promotion, yet the forces that allowed hashtags to become influential are deeply rooted in its conversational and sociable uses. The capacity of the hashtag to help people navigate real-time events such as disasters, protests, and conferences and to expand and solidify social connections and community proved particularly ideal for social movements and activism. Indeed, such uses have in many ways come to define both the hashtag and, increasingly, Twitter itself. Perhaps the most notable confluence of hashtags and bodies-in-the-street activism has come from #blacklivesmatter. As Freelon, McIlwain, and Clark document:

The Twitter hashtag was created in July 2013 by activists Alicia Garza, Patrisse Cullors, and Opal Tometi in the

wake of George Zimmerman's acquittal for second-degree murder of unarmed Black teenager Trayvon Martin. For more than a year, #Blacklivesmatter was only a hashtag, and not a very popular one: it was used in only 48 public tweets in June 2014 and in 398 tweets in July 2014. But by August 2014 that number had skyrocketed to 52,288, partly due to the slogan's frequent use in the context of the Ferguson protests. Some time later, Garza, Cullors, Tometi, and others debuted Black Lives Matter as a chapter-based activist organization.[11]

It's easy to dismiss hashtag activism as a form of slacktivism rather than real political engagement. But the rise of #blacklivesmatter and its material ties to street protests and unjust policing serves as an important reminder of the embodiment and liveness of many events that might look merely like "data" or verbal discourse when viewed as hashtags.

The real-time, ever-updating nature of Twitter made it particularly amenable to live-tweeting events such as the Ferguson protests as they happened, and hashtags proved ideal for organizing such tweets so that those participating either onsite or from afar could engage. In the next chapter, we will see, for instance, how people unable to help after the Boston bombing or unable to participate in the Occupy movement used the retweet feature to engage. This was only possible because of the hashtag. Zizi Papacharissi has shown in her book *Affective Publics* how hashtags serve as loci around which feelings and a sense of momentum build around acute events such as the 2011 Egyptian uprising and Occupy Wall Street protests.[12]

Disaster and political activism have proven significant cases for the hashtag, efforts Twitter has at times exploited in publicity materials, making the case for its own legitimacy. However, perhaps fortunately, most of the kinds of events live-tweeted by users are not crises, but more mundane. One of our interviewees, Fiona, noted the rise in hashtagging as she contrasted her experience live-tweeting a music festival in July 2009, when she realized there was only one other tweet with the event hashtag, with her experience a year later at the same event, when many more people were live-tweeting it. That they were doing so in many languages excited Fiona. By the time she went to an academic conference in 2011, the official coffee mugs had the conference hashtag on them, suggesting how widely incorporated into many events the hashtag had quickly become. Not all events provided an official hashtag, though, leading to some chaos around how to hashtag. Anne told us about going to a book fair. It was "a situation where there wasn't a hashtag, so I didn't really know what to do." Now the challenge tends not to be whether or not to have a hashtag, but which one it should be.

This sort of live-tweeting proved an asset to Twitter users who could not be present at an event but were interested in it, providing both a way to follow in real time and to catch up after the fact. Again, third-party platforms made this easier. The now-defunct add-on service Storify, for example, which compiled tweets into a linear series, organizing them into a narrative, was one particularly useful example. Bob, for instance, was not able to attend a professional event at which his company was presenting:

But I was able to watch everybody's tweets because everybody's using a hashtag. [. . .] So I made a Storify of this is what it looked like for somebody who wasn't there. They looked like they had a good time. As a—we wanted to put up a blog post on the website, but the actual blog posts—the person who's running the event wanted to wait some time before actually posting it. But we wanted to have some kind of capture of what happened during the event. So I made a Storify, threw it on there, and it was just an easy way to say, "yep, we did that thing. And here's some stuff that happened out of it. Come back to us in a month for more detailed commentary or whatnot."

Event live-tweeting also proved useful for those in attendance. Sonya told us about attending ROFLCon, a conference about internet culture, without knowing much about it. She described herself as sitting in sessions, tweeting and reading through TweetDeck, following the hashtag and gaining access to the kind of expertise and insider discourse that would otherwise have been opaque to her:

A lot of this I was hearing about for the first time, yet I was at this place where it was sort of an insider community, and I was reading about what the insiders were saying, and understanding what was going on around me, and then sort of hoping to add to the conversation there as well.

At events and outside of them, hashtags help to professionalize Twitter by fostering networking, though, in keeping with

Twitter's culture of sociability, often with a particularly personal, even intimate character. Fiona, for instance, used hashtags at conferences she attended as a way of creating a list of people she had met so that she could stay in touch with them: "I felt like I was part of a community, and it was really great." "The one thing I tend to lack on Twitter is friends," mused Sonya, so when she went to a conference with a hashtag, "I used Twitter strategically to cement connections with people that I'd met." "I thought if I meet people," she continued, "I could stay up to date with what they're doing professionally and things like that. Also it would be sort of like trading business cards."

These "serious" uses of the hashtag sit uneasily alongside, and sometimes arise from, more entertainment- and play-oriented practices. It is difficult to imagine #blacklivesmatter escalating as it did had "Black Twitter" not been well established already, in large part through creative, joyful uses of the hashtag feature. As Brock,[13] Florini,[14] and others have shown, early on Twitter was disproportionately popular among Black Americans, who found in it a mode of sociality that resonated with historical forms of language play, especially "signifyin'." This easy melding of existing community practice and technological affordance enabled "Twitter to mediate communal identities in near-real time; allowing participants to act individually yet en masse while still being heard."[15]

As Black Twitter demonstrates, hashtags can have a kind of ritual function. Some such rituals became embedded into Twitter's culture in their own right, becoming micro-features—e.g., #followfriday, reportedly established in 2009 by Micah Baldwin to enable users to introduce accounts to their followers that they might not know about already (and to get those accounts to notice them in the process).[16] The #auspol hashtag enabled collective griping—and antagonistic debate—about Australian politics. The #agchatoz hashtag (like its equivalents in other countries) engages a range of stakeholders in agriculture, agribusiness, and rural life in topical discussions, ideas sharing, and debates, and the community around it goes so far as to schedule a precisely weekly time and decide on discussion points in advance.[17] This is close to one of the original competing ideas for the purpose of the hashtag—to form channels or groups. The openness of Twitter, however, has meant that a range of interest groups and other hashtag conversations have collided in these weekly discussions, creating more dynamism and hybridity in the ad hoc publics it coordinates.

The role of the hashtag in developing "second screen" television watching, where people watch TV, follow the show's hashtag, and tweet together during the broadcast, is a notable sociable use of the hashtag that, like the use in protests that gained international coverage, helped to spread the hashtag beyond the Twitter platform into the broader media and offline ecosystems. Dayna Chatman's work on the hashtag for the television show *Scandal*, created by and starring African American women, shows how second-screen tweeting helped to create and affirm playful and fun community even as #blacklivesmatter rose.[18]

One of our interviewees, Anne, developed quite a liking for television hashtags, speaking of "getting into a groove" with them. Yet her reflections speak to the normative issues that even this sort of seemingly innocuous hashtag can raise. She described herself as intentionally not using the hashtag for *The Voice* both because of her intended and possible unintended audiences:

> I continued tweeting about *The Voice* because it turned out that I have coworkers who also watch it, and so we would tweet at each other and stuff like that. And so that was ultimately a way to connect with people that I knew in real life, and I think for the most part when I'm tweeting about *The Voice* with people I know I'm not using the *Voice* hashtag. I don't want Christina Milian to read my tweet aloud on the air like that.

Successful entertainment hashtags, in her view, could not be forced, saying it drives her crazy when television shows are

> trying too hard to make hashtags happen. I was watching an episode of *New Girl*, and there was a moment where somebody said something, and it was like a sort of funny turn of phrase, and immediately that phrase came up with a hashtag at the bottom. Why?

Anne's reluctance to accept prescribed hashtags hints at the tensions between the promotional culture of use hashtags encouraged with the sociable experience second-screen viewing was generally meant to be. In contrast, she found forced hashtags completely appropriate in professional contexts, in keeping with Twitter's emerging culture of professional use:

The #

I really appreciate going to conferences or things like that when there's an official hashtag so that if you're going to live-tweet everyone's using the same hashtag. Because often what I'll do is at different conferences if I can't go I'll search for that hashtag, and I'll read through and get all the live-tweeted stuff and stuff like that. So I really appreciate when that happens in a sort of real-life context if it's something that I'm actually wanting to connect to. But if you have a TV show the hashtag should be the name of your TV show and maybe a character or two, but it doesn't have to be, like, "joke hashtag." You don't have to delineate everything out, and I think that sometimes that happens and is ridiculous. [. . .] I just feel like that whole thing is sort of misguided.

Notably absent from the earliest hashtag archives are some of the expressive, exclamatory, and humorous uses of hashtags that are more familiar today. Nonetheless, driven by user creativity, hashtags quickly evolved into a means of making jokes or propagating funny memes. Florini, for instance, offers an analysis of the #fakedrakelyrics hashtag, which relied on deep enough familiarity with the musician Drake's stylistic habits to mock them, and presumed an audience of readers who shared that familiarity.[19] Sometimes, as Papacharissi has shown, hashtags that start as funny, such as #WhenIWas13, can evolve to simultaneously address serious issues. Lu and Steele discuss the celebration of Black children's joy through the hashtags #freeblackchild, #carefreeblackkids, and #CareFreeBlackKids2k16 on Twitter (and Vine) as a mode of engagement that is simultaneously joy-

ful and a means of resisting oppression.[20] Again, this points to
the entanglements between social, pleasurable uses of Twitter
and serious, political or newsworthy ones.

In addition people also began to use hashtags in ways that
entirely subverted the social organizing function of the sign,
serving instead to frame one's own tweets in humorous ways,
or to participate in playful conventions and memes. Hashtags
like #askingforafriend, used to wryly indicate you are "really" asking for yourself, do not organize topic, community,
or thread, and as such are both subversive and indicative
of users' ongoing creativity in the face of tightening formal
constraints.

Contestation

As our interview materials show, the hashtag remains a site of
uncertainty and conflict for users. Live-tweeting created new
problems. Live-tweeters worry about respecting the voices
(and experiences) of those they were citing in their tweets and
about flooding the feeds of those who don't care. Bob began
as a fairly enthusiastic live-tweeter, but moved to retweeting
at events instead, when he realized "well wait a minute, those
weren't my words but also if I do that I may be misrepresent-
ing what they're actually saying. So instead—so it's like a little
bit of like people who do that think of themselves as citizen
journalists or what not, and if they do it's really bad journalism, I decided."

Fiona worried about local social norms around live-tweeting
conferences for those present. "I was just at this conference
over the weekend in Europe," she told us, "and there's a fair

amount of hashtag activity, but I was live-tweeting the way I would always live-tweet, and apparently I'm far and away the most prolific tweeter at the entire conference. Somebody did a graphic, and I was kind of a little like, 'Oh God.' I felt a little self-conscious, like, 'Oh, did I just do something that was not okay in this context? Is European conference Twitter different?'" For Michelle, the idea of "being a conference twitterer" like Fiona "gagged" her. Why? Because she feared she would spend her time at the conference "trying to find the perfect thing to tweet so you could fit into the flow of it where you're just listening just to have something to tweet." "Live-tweeting can be a really great access tool for people who can't travel to every conference that they would want to go to," reflects Fiona, "but I also think there's some etiquette that can probably use some agreeing. Like, if we could all agree on sort of the rules of live-tweeting, I think that would probably help."

Others worried about flooding others' feeds with hashtags they did not care about, just as they had worried about @s directed to people their followers did not follow and, as we'll see in the next chapter, retweets in which they may not be interested. Daniel thought he would live-tweet more "if every Twitter application had a global filter like TweetDeck does," because "I would be much less worried about spamming people, especially on a hashtag. [. . .] If there were a hashtag mute button then I wouldn't care at all. I would just tag everything with that hashtag and leave it up to the user to decide to mute it or not, but the fact that the main basic Twitter client does not let you do that—it means that I need to be more cognizant of flooding people's Twitter feeds." Some people have responded to this by creating separate accounts just for live-tweeting, so they can steer interested followers to that account rather than flooding their regular feed. Others invite followers to unfollow for a few days while they live-tweet an event.

On the flip side of this, organized practices of flooding and manipulating hashtags have also grown into a problem. Since Twitter created trending topics, relying heavily on hashtags to do so, it drew attention to them in ways that inadvertently encouraged people to use the hashtag maliciously, either to add spam (advertisements, pornography) or, more troublingly, to engage in propoganda or organized attacks.[21] Gaming conferences, for example, almost made a sport of seeing how long a feminist could speak before trolls took over the hashtag.

As journalism and Twitter have become ever more conjoined, the early fusion of hashtags and journalistic framing, seen in #occupywallstreet and #blacklivesmatter, has become commonplace. Consider, for example, #metoo, based on the phrase first used by Tarana Burke to name a movement against sexual harassment long before Twitter, which later rose to public prominence through a Twitter hashtag, and is now widely used outside of Twitter to name a broad historical moment in which men are being called to account for harassment and worse sexual offenses. But these hashtags are ripe for invasion by outsiders (both human and bot) intending to disrupt and harm rather than share in community or work toward a common political goal. Far from being a way to connect people in discussion around a shared topic of interest (even if they didn't always agree), or a way to share up to-date information on a fast-moving event (even if the information wasn't always completely trustworthy), very high volume hashtags on controversial topics have now turned into cultural war zones.

Iteration

The hashtag is likely as unpopular with design purists as it was when Messina first proposed it to Twitter. From an aesthetic perspective, it is an inelegant and overly obtrusive element that clashes with the hegemony of "seamless" interface design according to which features should fade into the background so that they enable users to carry out their goals without needing to be aware of the technologies that enable their use. It is also open to annoying overuse by some social media marketers, who seem to feel the need to #hashtag #every #single #word #in #their #tweets While there have periodically been mutterings that it will be eliminated,[22] this seems unimaginable given the embeddedness of the hashtag in the vernaculars and grammars of social media across platforms.

The hashtag of today, though, is very far from the ideas about crowdsourced folksonomies of the Web 2.0 era, according to which the shape of the user community's collective interests would emerge over time, with the most popular hashtags referencing the most popular topics. The function of the hashtag as a way to surface topics and communities is now bound up with the Twitter search algorithm, which has an increasingly active curatorial role in major news and events in service of the apparently user-centered value of "relevance."[23] Hashtag publics are populated by bots and organizational accounts as well as individual human users. Trending topics, too, are algorithmically curated and moderated, partly to keep "fresh" hashtags at the top, and partly to counteract spam and other, usually automated, misuses of the hashtag feature.[24] But all of this happens behind the scenes—the search results for any particular hashtag still look like they represent all tweets that have included that hashtag. It is important to remember in studying or reporting on any hashtag "movement" or conversation that platforms actively filter and shape the conversations that are mediated by those hashtags. Thus, the story of the hashtag on Twitter, like the broader story of Twitter in this period of its life, might best be seen as one about a shift away from the coordination of ad hoc publics toward the representation of "calculated publics."[25]

3 The RT

If the @ and # features were responses to the problems of how to organize people, conversations, and topics on Twitter, the retweet feature responded to the dual problems of quoting people accurately and, increasingly important as Twitter grew and become a self-promotional environment, giving them (algorithmic) credit for their words. In everyday speech, we repeat others' words, often with introductions such as "then Jean said . . . ." In print, we use quotation marks to achieve the same effect. But with only 140 characters to spare for most of Twitter's history, and with both the @username and two quotation marks eating up valuable tweet real estate, attaining these normative standards was complex.

Appropriation

Unlike the @ and the #, there was no obvious single typographic convention to import from earlier forms of online

interaction. Historically, the problem had been handled in a variety of ways. Much writing, like this book, uses quotation marks. Usenet and early email clients, for instance, began lines with ">" to indicate that they were quoted from a prior message. As nonstandard punctuation has given way to the ideal of seamless interfaces, many email clients indicate quotation with color coding. In blogging, the trackback was an important technology for not only properly attributing an idea from another blog that you were referencing or arguing with, but also for automating that attribution in a way that "pinged" the blog in question, so that its author would be alerted of your post even if they weren't one of your regular readers. In this way, the trackback served as an attention-gaining as well as community-building mechanism.

Perhaps because there was no one symbol to appropriate, the retweet began with many more competing alternatives than @s or #s, each of which had nuances of their own. "Via" was first used in 2007 to grant attribution to another user, especially as a source of information or a link,[1] as in Jean's tweet from April that year:

> laughing at social media boardgame, via @tamaleaver http://tinyurl.com/2vu2sd

By the end of 2007, there were several alternatives in use: including HT (for hat tip), retweet, retweeting, and RT, as well as the Unicode recycling symbol (♺). As Farshad Kooti and co-authors describe, the users who innovated and first used these variations were atypical:

They posted more tweets, had higher network degree, and were more likely to describe themselves with words like "geek" and "founder"; in other words, they were the core members of the Twitter community.[2]

Early on, retweet conventions developed to distinguish between straight reposting, source attribution without quotation, and quotation or alteration of the original tweet. These were similar to formal academic conventions for citation, and indicated a sense that there was some kind of value-generating labor involved in the production of these very short posts that were becoming known as "tweets."

As the retweet began to spread throughout Twitter, participants learned it by watching others. But the range of options was, as is so often the case with Twitter, quite confusing. It took time to figure out what RT meant, let alone what the alternatives were and when each was most appropriate. At times, straight RTing did not work for users, especially given that indicating a tweet was an RT took valuable characters. This led to the MT (modified tweet) innovation.

As with the @, there was visible public pedagogy and discussion around the different alternatives and when you *should* use each variant.[3] A "better way to retweet," wrote one "expert," was to ask people to be creative and write their own tweet, but acknowledge the source with "via @user."[4] Fiona, one of our interviewees, was particularly concerned with identifying and adhering to the etiquette of using the variants correctly: "It's a lot of just kind of being in the environment and seeing what people are doing and kind of always being like, 'Okay, what are the social norms? What are the social norms?'" Retweeting, she found, was steeped in norms. "If somebody tweets something into my stream and I'm going to tweet from it, if there's room I usually try to squeak in a, like, 'via somebody,'" she told us, "because I feel like that's important. It's like citing, right?" But what about retweeting someone else's retweet? "Sometimes if it's just something someone retweeted and they didn't even alter it, I'm like, 'Do I really have to say via that person?' And I usually don't. I don't know if that's okay or not, but I temporarily decided for myself now that I guess it's okay." After months of seeing "MT" in her stream, she finally realized its utility in situations where one wants to keep the gist of the tweet, but not the exact wording. Once she realized this, she

> got very religious about changing to MT when I modify
> a tweet, right, to the point where I have actually
> responded to total strangers who I don't know when
> they have [manually] retweeted me and just radically
> altered what I've said. I've actually responded to them
> and been like, "Hey, so it'd be cool if you could say
> MT when you do that." I am that awful, rude person in
> a nice way. I try to be really nice about it, but it's just
> to the point where it's like, "You said that I said that,
> and I would never do a '4U' ever. Just no." I butcher
> the language in my own special way, like I'll turn a
> "would" into "WLD," "don't" or "do not" to "D/N." I'll do
> stuff like that, but I will not do the 4, I will not do the U.
> Standards, man. Standards.

Like Fiona, Anne was mortified to find one of her own tweets altered under the guise of being retweeted. Her tweet was about a television show and used a hashtag. A stranger, the first to retweet her, deleted a critical "ugh," totally changing the intended meaning. Fiona and Anne's comments demonstrate the complex displays of respect and identity at stake in this seemingly minor and innocuous feature, as well as the confusions that arose in the face of multiple, informal ways of handling the similar yet distinct issues of attribution and wording.

Incorporation

While confusing, contested, and disorganized, the practice of retweeting was becoming widely adopted, and embedded as part of Twitter's platform vernaculars. In early 2009, however, only the "RT" was still increasing in popularity. For Kooti et al., this demonstrated the power of early adopters and network effects in cementing one convention over other, perhaps "better," ones (like the use of the recycling symbol, for example).[5] In August 2009, Twitter announced that it would be building a "retweet" feature that would allow people to retweet by clicking a button available on all public tweets. In so doing, they hardwired RT as the official citation convention. This helped seal the ascendancy of those who favored Twitter as a serious mode of information transmission over those who favored it as a social platform, although, as we've seen, the former so often turns out to depend on the latter.

Highlighting the company's understanding of Twitter's co-creative characteristics, Biz Stone called the retweeting conven-

tion "a great example of Twitter teaching us what it wants to be."[6] The official announcement included a concept sketch showing that the original user's tweet would be preserved in its entirety when retweeted by another user, as in figure 3.1 below.

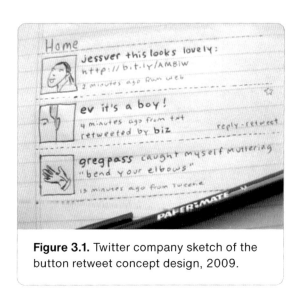

Figure 3.1. Twitter company sketch of the button retweet concept design, 2009.

In the company announcement, Stone acknowledged the user-led innovation that had generated the proof of concept and produced the need for the feature, while alluding to the tensions we have already seen between the insider knowledge needed to use Twitter's unique and quirky conventions and the need for user growth. Put simply, the syntax "RT @user" necessary to execute a retweet was obscure to new users:

Some of Twitter's best features are emergent—people inventing simple but creative ways to share, discover, and communicate. One such convention is retweeting. When you want to call more attention to a particular tweet, you copy/paste it as your own, reference the original author with an @mention, and finally, indicate that it's a retweet. The process works although it's a bit cumbersome and not everyone knows about it.

Retweeting is a great example of Twitter teaching us what it wants to be. The open exchange of information can have a positive global impact and the more efficient dissemination of information across the entire Twitter ecosystem is something we very much want to support. That's why we're planning to formalize retweeting by officially adding it to our platform and Twitter.com.[7]

Beginning in 2009 and rolled out worldwide as part of "New Twitter" in 2010, Twitter changed retweeting from a manual activity, embedding it into a function activated by simply pressing a "button" in the web version and official clients. This official retweeting protocol also displayed the tweet in its entirety, including the avatar of the account that posted the original tweet.

This was rolled out more carefully than it had been for @replies.[8] But still, the implementation of the retweet button was a tricky balancing act between competing user demands. In one sense the button retweet was a technological fix for fairly clear-cut user needs. It responded to concerns like Fiona's, around preserving the integrity of others' words and ensuring ideas were attributed to them. It addressed other issues as well. For example, prior to the RT button, it was easy to retweet a message from an account set to private. The button hardwired etiquette, making the retweet button unavailable and/or returning an error when people tried to retweet such messages.[9]

Although, as we'll see, the introduction of the button retweet function complicated the norm of preserving the integrity of the timeline, in some ways its incorporation attended to that concern by preventing multiple duplicate tweets. It wouldn't display a retweet to a user who was already following the account that posted the original tweet, or display the same retweet multiple times if posted by more than one of the accounts you were following.

This change also created a hard distinction between "quoting" and "retweeting" (one a later revision of the button would modify, as we discuss below); turning retweeting into simple redistribution of other people's content. For a detailed walkthrough of how this change worked and looked at rollout, see Bennett.[10] Twitter engaged in a fair amount of pedagogical and PR work around this change, both on and off the platform itself. "How to" stories, explainers, and Q&A sessions with tech journalists and developers prepared the ground.[11]

In one such post, co-founder Evan Williams wrote in his personal blog that the new feature should "make Twitter a more powerful system for helping people find out what's happening now that they care about,"[12] pointing to the mess and noise of the current manual form of retweeting and the problem of confused attribution. Incorporating RTs in this way served Twitter's business interests in making the platform more hospitable to new users, but like the other two features we have tracked, also conveniently served to make Twitter more datafiable and monetizable. Williams made it clear that part of the value proposition was in making retweets trackable—given their value as an indicator of resonance and attention, there was a thirst for metrics that could track and measure them. Just as the @, once embedded, provided a metric that could be used to determine and amplify "value," the RT offered a new metric more in line with advertising and media business logics than social networking site logics.[13] Before long, that metric, along with the number of likes and replies, were affixed by design to every tweet.

Williams's post clearly indicates that preserving both the early adopters' hacks and the more seamless and usable features aimed at new users was intentional:

> What about those cases where you really want to add a comment when RTing something? Keep in mind, there's nothing stopping you from simply quoting another tweet if that's what you want to do. Also, old-school retweets are still allowed, as well. We had to prioritize some use cases over others in this release. But just as Twitter didn't have this functionality at all before, people can still work around and do whatever they want. This just gives another option.[14]

Just as the @ became limited, so that you could no longer see @ replies directed at people you didn't follow, the remaking of the retweet offered the option of turning off retweets for accounts you followed.

As with the @, third-party clients handled RTs differently after the button implementation. The "RT @user [original tweet]" syntax had become normalized through use but was not

yet implemented in the Twitter platform or API. The original way of retweeting—manually composing a tweet with "RT @ user" at the beginning—became known as "organic" retweeting. Because people could still copy and paste text from the body of a tweet and were in the habit of doing so, it was still possible to retweet "organically" in most clients. With some third-party clients like Twhirl or TweetDeck it was possible to retweet with one click using a dedicated retweet button (usually marked with a ♻ recycling symbol), but website users (who accounted for most of the users at that time) needed to copy and paste the original tweet, and then add "RT @originaluser" to the beginning of it. For a time, an artefact of many users' persistent choice to manually retweet and the provision of this functionality in third-party clients was that the official mobile apps still allowed you to "quote" a tweet as well as to button retweet it or to manually type "RT [tweet text]."[15]

The implementation of the button helped make retweeting a mainstream mode of participating, solving some, but not all, of the normative issues around recirculating others' tweets. Some people came to see retweeting as a way of providing interesting content to their followers. One of the people we interviewed, for instance, maintained Twitter lists of people in his field that he would check regularly to see whether there was something interesting there to retweet. Retweeting created visibility, followers, and amplified attention. By incorporating the RT, Twitter hardwired in this promotional quality. Being retweeted became an event about which one was notified, and each tweet bore the mark of its success or failure as a retweetable tweet. Writing the tweets that others would retweet became a motivation for many. Sonya, a journalist, had been monitoring the ratio of her follower count to her tweeting frequency to assess the impact of her tweets. After a joke she told about a DNA computer, targeted at a "science-friendly audience," was widely retweeted, she saw her follower count grow. "And so then it was like, 'Okay, so dumb jokes work.'" She thus came to see an effective tweet as one that garnered retweets and brought new followers, and reshaped her practices in response.

Humor quickly emerged as a mode of sociable as well as professional retweeting. One of our interviewees, Daniel, made a variety of creative and humorous Twitter bots. When his bots' tweets were retweeted, he viewed himself as having contributed to Twitter's propensity toward humor: "My version of funny on Twitter is I make funny Twitter bots and then people retweet them." Our interviewee Nick initially used the RT almost exclusively to retweet jokes from novelty accounts such as @BronxZooCobra and @ModernDaySeinfeld. Anne, who particularly enjoys humorous hashtags, often retweeted funny tweets from such accounts:

> one I think that I retweeted [. . .] was @VeteranComic
> and it was—like, @VeteranComic says, "Our parents hit
> us and we turned out fine. Lives out of his car and seeks
> approval from strangers." You know, some of those
> things are where it's like, "Oh, yeah, that's good."

As @BronxZooCobra, @ModernDaySeinfeld, and @VeteranComic show, some Twitter users created not just humorous tweets, but

humorous accounts in hopes they would be retweeted. Some such joke accounts parlayed their visibility into book contracts and other monetizable ventures for their creators.

The influence of being retweeted was real. People began using RTs as a means of figuring out who was worth paying attention to. Fiona, for instance, would keep an eye on who was being retweeted at conferences she attended. After seeing someone retweeted a couple of times, she added them to a list that became her reading list. "Even people that I didn't meet at the conference, I would just throw them in on that list if it seemed like—if they were getting retweeted a bunch by people in my feed, saying things that I thought were cool."

As people came to see the value of being retweeted and began crafting tweets with intent to be retweeted, retweeting came to be implicitly regarded as a measure of quality. Sonya talked about a friendly competition with her colleagues at the magazine for which she wrote:

> The goal was to up your follower account, whichever time it was. The surefire way to do that was to get somebody with a higher follower account than you to retweet you. When we had our Twitter contest going on, I would try and be sort of snarkier, or get my tweet to be a tasty target for the company account to retweet.

It's worth noting here how the playful tweet came to facilitate the professional goals of upping follower counts at work, in much the same way that the hashtag blurred the line between newsworthy, serious Twitter and sociable, playful Twitter. But

figuring out exactly which tweets would make good retweets for others proved hard to predict, as Sonya said, "because I think there are times when people are actually reading Twitter and times when people aren't, and so it's hard to know who's reading you at what time."

Like Sonya, though even more so, Daniel began seeing the retweet as a "goal" when he tweeted. "I've definitely gotten better at setting goals for what I want my tweets to do and then making those happen," he told us. "I can write a tweet as almost like bait for someone else to RT and I know they'll see it and I'll sit there and wait and then yeah, five minutes later I see that they RTed it and I'm like, 'All right. That worked.'"

Retweets proved useful for promotion. Nick, who began his retweeting practices with humor, soon found that it was useful for promoting the community participation game he had been involved in creating:

> Our [game] was about to launch, so I was retweeting a
> lot of things from the official account, but also when we
> would get press or something I would retweet that to get
> more eyes on it. That was kind of one of my roles at [work],
> or I kind of took that as my role because I wanted people
> to know about our project.

Bob's first RT, in early 2009, was of himself, "retweeting my own account as a way to promote this other account I had." Daniel, who said he didn't generally make recommendations on Twitter, would break this rule, usually for "social obligations" like retweeting a friend's Kickstarter. "I wasn't really into it. I also didn't find it harmful and I was like, 'Well, okay.' I'll retweet it because it'll go to a lot of people and probably help them out."

Hashtags, we saw, helped organize serious news discussions and events. Retweeting became inextricable from this. When the Tsanarev brothers bombed the finish line of the Boston Marathon on a Monday afternoon, followed by a dramatic manhunt that shut down the city later in the week, Anne, frustrated at her inability to help directly, "retweeted a bunch of things, because I felt like I didn't have anything to add to the conversation, but I desperately wanted to." She explained how she chose what to retweet:

> I was glued to Twitter on Monday and then on Thursday, Friday, so I was getting all this information and especially, you know, all these actors were like, "Oh my God, donate blood. And retweet this. And give blood in Boston." And I was like, yeah that's not actually helpful. And so, like, my retweeting was "We don't need blood actually."

"So this is a suspension of your policy of not retweeting news that other people have probably seen?" we asked. "Yeah," she responded, "because I think that there's value in some of this news. Like, so police are telling people not to use their cell phones. Like if I retweet that, you know, maybe someone would see it and that would make a difference." Sometime later, when a gunman murdered a classroom full of kindergarten children and their teachers in Newtown, Connecticut, Anne again felt she wanted to add to the conversation, "but everyone is sad that children are dead. What can I add to it? So a retweet of information about gun violence, and then also the petition."

Similarly, Fiona, who had been active in the Occupy movement, wanted very much to remain involved in the protests but wasn't able to be present. She decided retweeting was a way to remain engaged by curating a trustworthy and useful live stream from the protests:

> Somebody would post something. And I'm trying to figure out is that probably true. Okay. And then search. So, the kind of curate then circulate process, and we would—my partner who I was living with at the time, we would both be up like four, five in the morning doing this. [. . .] It was sort of like, well, we're going to contribute to at least curating and circulating the information, trying to weed out the noise, and do the best we can to get what seems to be the best information out there. I was following Occupy Wall Street, Occupy Boston, Occupy San Francisco, and Occupy Oakland.

When, a few years later, tensions over police killings of unarmed Black men hit a boiling point in the United States, retweets, in coordination with the now famous hashtag, became crucial in building support for the Black Lives Matter movement.[16]

Contestation

The RT button was not immediately embraced by everyone. User Tim Whitlock developed a browser plugin that would reinstate an old-school RT button on the Twitter website,[17] invoking his desire to maintain the original "Twitter subculture" even as the platform was going "mainstream." Blogger Lisa Barone summed

up a number of such points of dissatisfaction in a post, arguing that the new retweet feature: put "strangers" in her stream; took away her ability to provide her own commentary; took away visibility in her own network; and, most importantly, through the technical implementation, the *definition and meaning* of retweeting was changed:

> Now when you retweet something, you're "liking it" the way you do on Facebook. You're not creating something new and of value, you're simply attaching your meta data to something that already exists. It's no longer a separate tweet.[18]

The button RT had been designed in part to preserve feed integrity by lessening repetition, but its very success came to challenge that integrity. The people we interviewed recalled a number of complaints about the introduction of the RT button. "I kind of didn't like seeing these random people I didn't know in my feed and I thought that was kind of odd," said one. "I was tweeting about how I didn't want that to be the new thing," said another. "I didn't like that on my feed there was people I didn't know, like the pictures popping up, like, 'Who is that? Why are they in my feed?'" Feeds filled with the tweets of strangers, and sometimes, it is true, their posts were not interesting. The strangers, even when interesting, could also overwhelm, all but forcing you into following people you had not chosen to follow. "I blocked the guy who made Minecraft," one of our interviewees told us, "not out of any ill will towards him, but he has so many Twitter followers. My entire stream would be game developers I know retweeting stuff that he's said and the easiest way to mute that was to just block him and that way I don't see retweets from him anymore." In some cases, like Black Twitter, RTing made performances of racial, ethnic, and other social identities newly visible to people who might otherwise have imagined a more homogeneous Twitter.

The range of competing technical possibilities generated much discussion about how to retweet properly, revealing conflicting norms among diverse communities of users. For quite a while, there was discussion about the pros and cons of both manual and automated methods, because both remained technically possible.[19] But as the button retweet became normalized, *Buzzfeed*'s Katie Notopoulos reported, "manual RT shaming" became common. Notopoulos explained how this was tied to the algorithmic benefits of the button RT's attribution:

> The ire comes from two places. Firstly, a manual retweet in a way claims someone else's tweet as your own—sort of a Twitter version of putting your watermark logo on someone else's photo. Secondly, a manual RT robs the original tweeter of potential retweets and favorites. By manually RTing, you're bogarting the favs, man.[20]

Similarly, our interviewee Fiona described a friend of hers who resented manual retweets "because it moves the metrics onto you rather than them." She found it interesting that her peers maintained these social norms:

> But it is kind of like an etiquette thing, and, yeah, I sometimes wonder when I tweet and it'll be either a

retweet and I'll add something ahead of it or I'll modify
it so I can say something—sometimes I really have
something to say, and other times it's just like, "Ha. This
is funny," and I'm like, "Is that okay? I don't know if that's
okay. Am I cheating? Am I stealing your social whatever?"

Here we can see a reflexive but uncertain consideration of the ethics of sharing and attribution on Twitter—Fiona is concerned about the etiquette of getting attention by sharing content that was first shared by others. The uneasiness here seems to be partly about interpersonal respect, but it may also result from social media becoming increasingly inflected with ideas (like intellectual property and audience metrics) that originally come not from the conventions of personal communication, but from the media and advertising industries.

Retweets are now one of the most significant metrics of attention and success on the platform. The button retweet made tracking (and monetizing) attention far easier, and third-party services jumped in to provide metrics services to suit. Favstar.fm, for example, emerged to track retweets and likes on popular tweets or, for a fee, to provide detailed information on how often and by whom one's own tweets were shared by others. Klout created proprietary algorithms to determine which individuals on various social media platforms were "influencers." After the launch of "New Twitter," they were easily able to use retweets (as well as follower counts) as one measure of influence, and hence social status.

Attention and engagement metrics are important not only to media, advertising, and brand communication businesses, but also for both professional and amateur creative users (especially

comedy performers and writers) who use Twitter to distribute or perform original material and for whom both copyright ownership of their material and ability to measure attention (whether through retweets or "favstars") is materially important. Following an acute series of controversies over "stolen tweets" (tweets reposted without attribution), Twitter demonstrated that it was willing to respond by introducing copyright-violation flagging mechanisms. Both the controversy and the official response to it showed how far Twitter had traveled from being a social networking service to being a media platform,[21] and how, for some users, community norms had followed this path. The below (partly humorous) tweet, for example, points to the superior value of (public) retweeting to (more privately) offering likes (or "stars"—now, despite predictable user outcry, replaced by hearts); similarly, button retweets, which preserve attribution, are better than manual RTs, which may not link back to the original user. For the creative communities associated with comedy Twitter, passing off another user's tweets as your own is almost the worst sin you could commit, second only to the purchase of "fake" followers in its immorality.

Twitter Etiquette, Best to Worst:
1. stars + RT's
2. stars only
3. no stars or RT's
4. manual RT's
5. stealing tweets
6. buying followers
—snowjob (@canadasandra)[22]

Notably, the rise of the stolen tweet and the purchase of followers, the last two items on this list, both speak to the emerging strategies for gaming Twitter that followed in the wake of its moves to create more attention metrics, including the rise of "retweet cartels."[23] Coordination outside of Twitter to amplify some voices rather than others also became a game of sorts, one with significant consequences. Media outlet Politico, for instance, reported on the "secret Twitter rooms of Trump nation" leading up to the 2016 US presidential election in which small groups of Trump supporters coordinated to boost some messages and hashtags through mass retweeting.[24]

The life stories of platforms play out through the countless tiny decisions people make in their everyday lives about how to use them. Twitter users responded to the problem of flooding others' feeds with retweets they may or may not appreciate by developing highly personalized rules about how often and what kinds of tweets they retweet to their own followers. Daniel, one of our interviewees, tried not to retweet more than two tweets in a row, although there were exceptions:

> Sometimes I'll be involved in a big discussion with a
> lot of people and I'll get some really good responses
> and so I'll tweet three or four or five even of the really
> good responses or if I ask a question on Twitter—that's
> something I do a lot. I'll ask a question. "Hey, what's an
> example of a great to-do list application for managing your
> tasks?" and so people will respond and then I'll usually RT
> the answers so people who were following that can see
> how that conversation went. But generally speaking, yeah.

> I try not to over-RT, for some definition of "over" that is
> very loose and contextual.

Bob began to "self-censor" his RTs, particularly those that he thought could fan the flames of flamewars. "With game development," he told us, "it's always like someone said stupid thing X and so someone tweets about it and someone responds to it. And then someone misunderstands another person and then they misunderstand that person. Their friends come in and then it gets retweeted and then it just goes like wildfire." Anne initially chose not to retweet at all, feeling that if she had seen something on Twitter, surely those who followed her would have as well. Over time, that changed, though her retweeting practices remained rule based, with the self-imposed dictate that she try to be productive, particularly in the wake of national tragedies.

Users continue to struggle with the competing norms about whether retweeting is a good or a bad thing in different contexts, as well as with their very different ideas about what is worth retweeting. But, in 2019, it is less usual and indeed very cumbersome to perform manual RTs, because of the dominance of official Twitter clients (apps) and because many of these apps discourage (or outright disable) the copying and pasting of text within tweets, and encourage the button retweet instead. Despite their initial resistance, our interviewees, like most users, generally came to accept and even prefer the button RT. "I was really against it," Nick told us "and then I slowly, slowly started. It was just so easy, just don't have enough time to rewrite everything and copy-paste it." What's more, Nick came to appreciate other affordances of the new button. He points to a retweet he did of the account @FakeAPStylebook. "Maybe here I think to me it made sense that I would retweet it, because without the context of Fake AP Stylebook you wouldn't get the joke, so I think there I found some instances where I thought it would be good." He points to another button RT in his archive: "And then maybe here I think there too it's like there's some things either that wouldn't fit, you couldn't tweet the whole thing if you didn't use their thing, or also you didn't want it to come from you."

Bob used to use "via," but found the many possible forms of manual retweets too complex. The button was easier than thinking "about the RT or the HT. Am I going to change their words? If I'm going to change their words, am I just taking out a preposition? Does it have to be—what exactly is going on here?" He also came to appreciate the way the button retweet preserved the integrity of other speakers' voices:

> [It's] actually a better way of retweeting I think than the RT. [. . .] It's the actual voice of the other person. You're not modifying it. You're not adding comment to it. If you want comment, you put on the tweet afterwards, which is actually—sometimes I would love to be able to annotate it. I wish there was a way to just add my comment to it that other people would see. But this feels more respectful to the other person.

Furthermore, the market share of third-party alternative clients that *did* supply alternatives to the button retweet is dramatically diminished since Twitter bought and converted the leading clients for most devices into their official clients, which obey its user experience and display rules consistently. It was possible in April 2019 to copy the text of a tweet displayed in the browser, once you clicked on the tweet from within the timeline to open it in a popup window. But for the vast majority of user experience scenarios, each tweet is treated as an inviolable media object with one author (the original account) rather than as an open text. Doing a manual or modified tweet these days, on most Twitter apps, requires the manual transcription of the original tweet. It's too much trouble for most users.

Saving the user the trouble in this case also worked to convert tweets from ephemeral status updates to media objects (or items of "content") that were more clearly owned by and attributed to particular users (including corporate users like news organizations), and a particularly valuable form of engagement with these media objects (sharing with attribution) could now more easily be measured. This shift was also core to the company's business model, as the platform sought to become a media- and advertiser-friendly channel. By preserving authorial attribution, it fed into the preservation of intellectual property native to media logic, and by fostering the retweet as an incentive and marker of quality, helped to create a culture of serious use at odds with the conversational and interpersonal ethos of some users.

Iteration

Once embedded, the RT continued to evolve as users and the site's developers responded to each other's moves. The "retweet with quote" feature introduced in 2015 allows users to comment

on and annotate a tweet on top of retweeting it—but still not to *selectively* quote or edit it;[25] as of April 2019, it was also possible to retweet your own tweets or replies.[26]

In sum, we see with the RT a path quite similar to those of the @ and the #. Users see a need—in this case attribution combined with saving precious character space. They develop strategies to address it, resulting in confusion about best practices. The site intervenes by incorporating one strategy into its structure. This results in ongoing contestation over how to do it "right" and, perhaps more perniciously, nudges people toward creating messages that will circulate widely, rewarded by attention and engagement metrics. And the nudges seem to have worked: as button retweeting is ever more encouraged by the platform's design and affordances, retweets have come to dominate the usage of the platform over both original tweets and replies,[27] making Twitter more newsy, more noisy, and less conversational than it was in its youth.

Conclusion

Over the past three chapters, we've told the origin stories of three of Twitter's most distinctive native features: the @, the hashtag, and the retweet. They're not three separate stories, though; they are one. They're the story of Twitter, in this early phase of its formation, between 2006 and 2009, when it was ambiguous, experimental, playful, and filled with potential, yet on the path to becoming the status-seeking and serious, if troubled, platform it became. The three features emerged around the same time, in the same milieu, and followed relatively similar pathways as they evolved. From the platform biography perspective of this short volume, our goal has been to reveal the dynamic interplays between different actors that lie behind these pathways, which might otherwise be read as natural, progressive developments.

In each of the three cases on which we have focused, a set of conventions emerged through user experimentation, as people appropriated symbols and practices from elsewhere and competed to concretize the platform's emerging uses and norms in particular ways. In some cases, lead users and third-party developers created new tools to enhance and better coordinate these conventions. Different sets of users with different practical solutions in effect competed in an origin period of relative interpretative flexibility—a concept that van Dijck[1] borrows from the social construction of technology literature[2] and applies to social media platforms—with the platform playing catch-up, trying to keep pace with and also influence its users' practices, which gradually shifted toward more consistent and, therefore, more measurable and monetizable practices.

Eventually, lead users, in conjunction with the media whose attention they are able to elicit, won the day and Twitter incorporated each practice as a *feature* that was both built into the front-end interface and connected to back-end data infrastructures and operations. In doing so, the company inevitably privileged some logics over others. Far from being settled at that point, a third phase of ongoing yet renewed contestation followed in which people continued to experiment, both adopting and pushing back against how Twitter has institutionalized the features. Competing norms and design ideas lived on in features even after they were embedded. In a fourth phase, Twitter iterates, and contestation continues.

Looking closely at features helps us to see how Twitter is organized, in whose interests, and how these arrangements have changed over time. We might think of the early childhood of Twitter as we have depicted it as a time when squabbling siblings struggled over whether Twitter's purpose was informa-

+ Conclusion

tion or conversation, publicity or personal connection. The struggles over norms at play in the emergence of the @, the hashtag, and the retweet set the stage for the Twitter we have now, with its global scale and astonishingly diverse userbase, as well as its damaging proliferation of spam, disinformation, and abuse. Features that enable popular participation also enable large-scale exploitation. What began as a me-centered culture of sociality, in which people announced what they were doing primarily to people they knew, largely lost out to the culture of global news and professionalism. The still-emerging idea of a public space that had once been represented by a global feed showing all tweets posted to the service became something more personalized, measured, and targeted, and simultaneously more organized around media industry advertising logics than interpersonal communication.

As it aged and grew, Twitter also stopped encouraging feral, organic third-party innovation and turned toward centralization, business maturity, and both technical and organizational enclosure. As we discussed in the introduction, not only did the Twitter APIs and other infrastructural elements become less freely accessible to external developers and researchers, but the company culture as reflected in its external communications also became far more controlled. While on the one hand these processes of enclosure are perhaps a natural consequence of business maturity in a highly competitive market, they also work as a shield against community protest, external scrutiny, and public oversight or regulation.

As we have shown, a key characteristic of Twitter's maturity is the close integration of its user features with advertising-driven attention metrics and a data- and media-centered business model. These media logics and metrics fuel the sense that the platform matters, that what happens there is to be taken seriously. At the same time, the service's emphasis on attention and engagement as measures of the value and influence of individual users and their "content" creates incentives for people to participate in more media-centered ways. Why waste your time chatting sociably with friends when you can become an influencer, with the followers and retweet numbers to prove it? In late 2018, with Twitter still unable to climb out from under the widespread perception that it is riddled with problems, Jack Dorsey himself mused that perhaps Twitter's metrics of attention, such as the "like" button, were partly to blame. In a move that would have upended the informal economy of Twitter, he reportedly contemplated erasing visible tweet metrics from the interface entirely.[3]

The very category of "user" became more complex over the course of Twitter's youth, as the changes we've explored opened doors to large-scale exploitation, most notably from non-human agents (bots) tweeting as if they were real. While some bots are creative and fun, and even spam may be experienced as merely an annoyance, other non-human agents are deliberately made to appear human and muddy the waters of public discourse, with very real consequences, as is the case with bots created by Russian agents to inflame racial tensions in the United States and help elect Trump.[4] Considered against the backdrop of world politics, clearly the features we have described cannot be blamed for all of Twitter's woes, but they have played a crucial role—and by tracing how they have changed over time, we have been able to see more clearly how Twitter and the wider society have co-evolved.

Beyond Twitter

The picture of Twitter that we have painted is, of course, incomplete. This is a short book, intended as a proposal for a new and accessible approach to studying platforms, not as the final word on one particular platform. No biography captures everything, but pursued systematically and over time, the method offers an elegant way to make sense of complex histories. The overarching approach is this: take a platform, conceived as the intersection of technology, design, business models, and cultures of use; and then tell the story of those intersections and how they have shifted, reconstructing the histories of key, platform-specific features using available materials, and conducting oral history interviews with users who are able to reflect on their own changing experiences of using the platform.

For instance, we can imagine the life story of Facebook being told through the history of the newsfeed, or the "like" button;[5] or perhaps, as Helmond, Nieborg, and van der Vlist[6] have modeled already, the changing configuration of the company's corporate and infrastructure partnerships as it evolved from social networking site to platform. Similarly, the life story of Spotify might be told through the playlist; the story of YouTube through its video and channel discovery and recommendation systems, or its protocols for copyright control. One might turn to consider the absence of features as well, like, in the case of Twitter, the much-desired ability to edit tweets (which users have called for over and over again but which has not been forthcoming),

Conclusion

and the need for a "report abuse" button, which was only recently added, in response to user activism.

Whatever the focal points or analytical techniques, the platform biography approach aims to do justice to the ways that, as long as they're still alive, platforms—just like humans—are always becoming, never fully grown, and their development is never just technical, but also social in character. Integrating user interviews is an important counterbalance to the equally necessary focus on mechanics, data infrastructures, and interfaces that could otherwise overwhelm platform studies. We have shown that users have always been reflexive in choosing among different interpretations and practices alongside changing technology. Interviews, particularly those in which users are able to reflect on their own archives, give us otherwise unattainable insights into how the story of any platform is one of real people going about their lives, running into challenges with how platforms work, and coming up with workarounds to manage those challenges. Some of these user conventions become embedded as features, but many alternative options don't, leaving potentially valuable community innovations on the sidelines. Users' recollections of changing practices also reveal how porous Twitter's cultures of use have been to surrounding social norms and people's lives and relationships, as well as responding to and influencing broader social and political developments.

Closing Thoughts

Twitter used to be fun. It felt like a wide-open space marked by ambiguity and a spirit of creativity. Users understood it to be for them, and went to work organizing it in ways that aligned with their lives, their communities, and their values. As Twitter adopted and embedded the users' tools in very particular ways, the platform features that resulted subtly but profoundly altered not only the culture of Twitter, but also the structures and dynamics of the media environment more broadly.

The challenge, for Twitter and for other platforms, is maintaining a tension between generativity (the ability to transform and do new things with features) and usability (the ease of grasping what a feature is for and doing things with it that are in your interests). Too far one way, and nobody but insiders and early adopters understand the platform's conventions; too far the other way, and the possibilities for use become too constrained and the features become static, unable to be changed or used differently. The challenge for all of us is how to maintain the creative power users have to reshape the cultures of digital media platforms, especially when they seem to be veering precipitously toward interests that may work against their users' security, privacy, well-being, and civic agency.

One source of hope, however small, may lie in Twitter's origins. We have seen throughout this book that even the serious uses toward which Twitter has been put build upon its culture of sociability. Yet that sociability has too often been dismissed as trivial, "pointless babble," or simply not particularly newsworthy. As Jessica Lu and Catherine Knight Steele note, "provocations of joy meant to remain in-group do not incite Twitter wars or debates that journalists could bill as indicative of the mood of the nation."[7] Community cultural expressions are less likely than political arguments and protests to be taken seriously by journalists (and, in many cases, by academic researchers). But by downplaying the pleasurable, popular, and everyday, and instead paying disproportionate attention to more obviously political debates, conflicts, and controversies, we amplify antagonism and political polarization, all the while feeding social media platforms' engagement metrics. Can Twitter's culture be turned around, and transformed into the space for "healthy conversation" that the company says it wants?[8]

Well, where there's life, there's hope. If we really want to improve the health of social media, we can learn from early Twitter the power of a balanced mixture of intimate, everyday communication and news of the world at large; and we can learn from Black Twitter the power of joy as resistance. By holding on to and choosing to amplify joyful expression, play, and sociable intimacy, we may yet find ways to reaffirm and rediscover the positive power of social connection that digital media platforms continue to afford—if only we can hear each other over the noise.

Acknowledgments

Microsoft Research New England's Visiting Researcher program provided Jean with the opportunity to spend several months with the Social Media Collective there, and for Nancy and Jean to design the project, conduct the interviews, and collect much of the archival material on which the book is based. A Queensland University of Technology (QUT) New Professor's Grant provided Jean with funding for research assistance.

We are grateful to the research participants who gave so much of their time, opened up their Twitter archives to us, and shared with us the many fascinating ways the stories of their own lives had come to be entangled with Twitter's.

We received invaluable research assistance from Kate Miltner, Andrea Alarcon, Sarah Hamid, and Christopher Persaud at Microsoft Research, and from Dr. Kim Osman at QUT.

We thank all our colleagues and friends in the Microsoft Research Social Media Collective, the QUT Digital Media Research Centre (DMRC), the 2017 DMRC Summer School participants, and the Association of Internet Researchers community for their insightful feedback, probing questions, and the rich source of inspiration their own work provides.

Notes

Introduction

1 Twitter, 2017.
2 The Google Scholar search query we used is "intitle:Twitter." For the purpose of comparison, on the same day the search results indicated that "YouTube" appeared in the title of 13,200 articles and "Facebook" appeared in the title of 79,600 articles.
3 Murthy, 2012; Weller et al., 2014.
4 McGregor and Molyneux, 2018; Murthy, 2018.
5 Murthy, 2018; Vieweg et al., 2010.
6 Douglas, 2007.
7 Glaser, 2007.
8 Needleman, 2007.
9 Kottke, 2007.
10 See, for example, Glaser, 2007.
11 Zittrain, 2008.
12 Glaser, 2007.
13 Brock, 2012: 538.
14 Sweet, Pearson, and Dudgeon, 2013.
15 Sniderman, 2010.
16 Zara, 2018; Grigonis, 2018.
17 Miller, 2009.

18   Miller, 2009.
19   Burgess and Bruns, 2015.
20   Bilton, 2014: loc. 984.
21   Reichelt, 2007.
22   Bilton, 2014: loc. 3203.
23   Stone, 2009b.
24   Kelly, 2009.
25   Arceneaux and Weiss, 2010.
26   Marwick and boyd, 2009.
27   Papacharissi and Easton, 2013.
28   Burgess, 2015a.
29   See Lu and Steele, 2019; Monk-Payton, 2017.
30   Brügger, 2018.
31   Van Dijck, 2013: 19.
32   Hallinan and Striphas, 2016.
33   Crawford and Gillespie, 2016.
34   Postigo, 2016.
35   Bucher, 2012.
36   Burgess and Green, 2009.
37   Burgess and Green, 2018.
38   Van Dijck, 2013.
39   A proposition that is laid out most cogently in van Dijck and Poell, 2013.
40   Altheide and Snow, 1979.
41   Williams, 1974.
42   Van Dijck and Poell, 2013: 3.
43   Ibid.: 6.
44   LaFrance and Meyer, 2014.
45   Rogers, 2014.
46   Van Dijck, 2013: 68–69.
47   Ibid.: 6.
48   Ibid.
49   Ibid.: 7.
50   Ibid.: 10.
51   Van Dijck, 2008.
52   Banks, 2012.
53   Van Dijck, 2013.
54   Neff and Stark, 2003.
55   Acker and Beaton, 2016: 1891.

56 Ibid.

57 Joy, 2009.

58 Appadurai, 1998.

59 Du Gay et al., 1997.

60 See, for example, Arceneaux and Weiss, 2010; boyd, Golder, and Lotan, 2010; Honeycutt and Herring, 2009; Kooti et al., 2012; Marwick and boyd, 2011.

61 Bolton, 2014.

62 The Wayback Machine can be accessed at https://archive.org/web.

63 Gibbs et al., 2016; Kennedy, Meese, and van der Nagel, 2016.

64 Hartley, Burgess, and Green, 2007.

65 See, for example, Stocks, 2016.

66 Efrati, 2011.

67 Galloway, 2004.

68 Van Dijck and Poell, 2013.

69 Bucher, 2013.

70 Serres, 1995.

Chapter 1. The @

1 Quoted in Miller, 2009.

2 Dom's "@errand" tweet is here: https://twitter.com/dom/status/83.

3 Sagolla, 2012.

4 Ev's breakfast burrito tweet is here: https://twitter.com/ev/statuses/327.

5 Jack's "at work" status update is here: https://twitter.com/jack/statuses/463.

6 Murray, 2012.

7 Anderson's tweet "@ buzz . . ." is here: https://twitter.com/rsa/status/55281.

8 Honeycutt and Herring, 2009.

9 Stone, 2007.

10 Ibid.

11 See, for example, Dimmick, 2003; McVeigh-Schultz and Baym, 2015; Madianou and Miller, 2012.

12 Reproduced in Henshaw-Plath, 2012.

13 The command "D" (for "direct") followed by "@username" was used to send private messages.

14 Reichelt, 2007.

15 Halavais, 2014: 33.

16 Meyer, 2007.

17 Stone, 2009a.

18 Ibid.

19 Halavais, 2014: 34.

20 Parr, 2009a.

21 Stone, 2009a.

22 Sherman, 2016.

Chapter 2. The

1 Marlow et al., 2006.

2 Ibid.

3 Messina, 2007a, 2007b.

4 Cooper, 2013.

5 Bilton, 2014: loc. 1664.

6 Messina, 2007a, 2007b; Gannes, 2010.

7 The Hashtags.org page is archived at the Internet Archive, where it is accessible via the Wayback Machine (https://archive.org/web).

8 Rao, 2009.

9 Bruns and Burgess, 2015.

10 Rambukkana, 2015.

11 Freelon, McIlwain, and Clark, 2016.

12 Papacharissi, 2015.

13 Brock, 2012.

14 Florini, 2014.

15 Brock, 2012: 539.

16 Baldwin, 2009.

17 Burgess, Galloway, and Sauter, 2015.

18 Chatman, 2017.

19 Florini, 2014.

20 Steele, 2019.

21 See, for example, Trice and Potts, 2018.

22 See Ulanoff, 2014.

23 Gillespie, 2104.

24 Duguay, 2018.

25 Bruns and Burgess, 2015.

Chapter 3. The RT

1 Kooti et al., 2012.

2 Ibid.

3 Parr, 2009b.

4 Tinsley, 2009.

5 Kooti et al., 2012.

6 Stone, 2009c.

7 Ibid.

8 Halavais, 2014: 35.

9 Ibid.

10 Bennett, 2009.

11 For a good example, see Catone, 2009.

12 Williams, 2009.

13 Ibid.

14 Ibid.

15 Halavais, 2014: 36.

16 Freelon, McIlwain, and Clark, 2016.

17 Whitlock, 2010.

18 Barone, 2009.

19 Bransford, 2011.

20 Notopoulus, 2013.

21 Khan, 2015.

22 The "Twitter Etiquette" tweet is here: https://twitter.com/canadasandra/status/322014310945652737.

23 Paßmann, Boeschoten, and Schäfer, 2014.

24 Musgrave, 2017.

25 Shu, 2015.

26 The "retweet with quote" is not to be confused with the old "quote" feature on some third-party clients, which placed a copy of the original tweet into a new tweet for editing.

27 Burgess, 2015a.

Conclusion

1 Van Dijck, 2013.

2 For example, Pinch and Bijker, 1984.

3 Byager, 2018.

4 Howard, Woolley, and Calo, 2018.

5 See, for example, Gerlitz and Helmond, 2013.

6 Helmond, Nieborg, and van der Vlist, 2019.

7 Lu and Steele, 2019: 834.

8 See Lu and Steele, 2019; Harvey and Gasca, 2018.

 Notes

References

Acker, Amelia, and Brian Beaton. 2016. "Software Update Unrest: The Recent Happenings around Tinder and Tesla." *49th Hawaii International Conference on System Sciences*. IEEE. DOI: 10.1109/HICSS.2016.240.

Altheide, David L., and Robert P. Snow. 1979. *Media Logic*. Beverly Hills, CA: SAGE.

Appadurai, Arjun, ed. 1988. *The Social Life of Things: Commodities in Cultural Perspective*. Cambridge: Cambridge University Press.

Arceneaux, Noah, and Amy S. Weiss. 2010. "Seems Stupid until You Try It: Press Coverage of Twitter, 2006–9." *New Media & Society* 12(8): 1262–1279.

Baldwin, Micah. 2009. "#FollowFriday: The Anatomy of a Twitter Trend." *Mashable*, 6 March. http://mashable.com.

Banks, John. 2012. "The iPhone as Innovation Platform: Reimagining the Videogames Developer." In Larissa Hjorth, Jean Burgess, and Ingrid Richardson, eds., *Studying Mobile Media: Cultural Technologies, Mobile Communication, and the iPhone* (pp. 155–172). New York: Routledge.

Barone, Lisa. 2009. "Why Twitter's New Retweet Feature Sucks." *Outspoken Media*, 18 November. http://outspokenmedia.com.

Bennett, Shea. 2009. "Twitter's Project Retweet Goes Live—Let's Take a Closer Look." *Adweek*, 10 November. https://www.adweek.com.

Bilton, Nick. 2014. *Hatching Twitter*. London: Hodder & Stoughton. Kindle.

boyd, danah, Scott Golder, and Gilad Lotan. 2010. "Tweet, Tweet, Retweet: Conversational Aspects of Retweeting on Twitter." *43rd Hawaii International Conference on System Sciences*. IEEE. DOI: 10.1109/HICSS.2010.412.

Bransford, Nathan. 2011. "Should You Use RT or the Retweet Button on Twitter?" Personal blog, 31 May. http://blog.nathanbransford.com.

Brock, André. 2012. "From the Blackhand Side: Twitter as a Cultural Conversation." *Journal of Broadcasting & Electronic Media* 56(4): 529–549.

Brügger, Niels. 2018. "Web History and Social Media." In Jean Burgess, Alice Marwick, and Thomas Poell, eds., *SAGE Handbook of Social Media* (pp. 196–212). Los Angeles and London: SAGE.

Bruns, Axel, and Jean Burgess. 2015. "The Use of Twitter Hashtags from Ad Hoc to Calculated Publics." In Nathan Rambukkana, ed., *Hashtag Publics* (pp. 13–28). New York: Peter Lang.

Bucher, Taina. 2012. "Want to Be on the Top? Algorithmic Power and the Threat of Invisibility on Facebook." *New Media & Society* 14(7): 1164–1180.

———. 2013. "Objects of Intense Feeling: The Case of the Twitter APIs." *Computational Culture* 3. http://computationalculture.net.

Burgess, Jean. 2015a. "From 'Broadcast Yourself' to 'Follow Your Interests': Making Over Social Media." *International Journal of Cultural Studies* 18(3): 281–285.

———. 2015b. "Twitter (Probably) Isn't Dying, but Is It Becoming Less Sociable?" *Medium—DMRC at Large*, 6 November. https://medium.com/dmrc-at-large.

Burgess, Jean, and Axel Bruns. 2015. "Easy Data, Hard Data: The Politics and Pragmatics of Twitter Research after the Computational Turn." In Ganaele Langlois, Joanna Redden, and Greg Elmer, eds., *Compromised Data: From Social Media to Big Data* (pp. 93–111). London: Bloomsbury.

Burgess, Jean, Anne Galloway, and Theresa Sauter. 2015. "Hashtag as Hybrid Forum: The Case of #agchatoz." In Nathan Rambukkana, ed., *Hashtag Publics: The Power and Politics of Discursive Networks* (pp. 61–76). New York: Peter Lang.

Burgess, Jean, and Joshua Green. 2009. *YouTube: Online Video and Participatory Culture*. Cambridge: Polity Press.

———. 2018. *YouTube: Online Video and Participatory Culture*. 2nd edition. Cambridge: Polity Press.

Byager, Laura. 2018. "Twitter Is Reportedly Removing the 'Like' Button and People Do Not Like It." *Mashable*, 29 October. https://mashable.com.

Calore, Michael. 2009. "Much Ado about Reply." *Wired*, 13 May. www.wired.com.

Catone, Josh. 2009. "HOW TO: Use Twitter's New Retweet Feature." *Mashable*, 22 November. http://mashable.com.

Cederholm, Dan. 2006. "Reasons I Like Twitter." *SimpleBits*, 20 December. http://vault.simplebits.com.

Chatman, Dayna. 2017. "Black Twitter and the Politics of Viewing Scandal." In Jonathan Gray, Cornel Sandvoss, and C. Lee Harrington, eds., *Fandom: Identities and Communities in a Mediated World* (pp. 299–314). New York: New York University Press.

Cooper, Belle Beth. 2013. "The Surprising History of Twitter's Hashtag Origin and 4 Ways to Get the Most out of Them." *Buffer—Social Blog*, 24 September (updated 19 April 2016). https://blog.bufferapp.com.

Crawford, Kate, and Tarleton Gillespie. 2016. "What Is a Flag For? Social Media Reporting Tools and the Vocabulary of Complaint." *New Media & Society* 18(3): 410–428.

Denton, Nick. 2006. "A Website about Nothing." *Gawker*, 22 December. http://gawker.com.

Dimmick, John. 2003. *Media Competition and Co-existence: The Theory of the Niche*. Mahwah, NJ: Lawrence Erlbaum Associates.

Douglas, Nick. 2007. "Twitter Blows Up at SXSW Conference." *Gawker*, 12 March. http://gawker.com.

Du Gay, Paul, Stuart Hall, Linda Janes, Hugh Mackay, and Keith Negus. 1997. *Doing Cultural Studies: The Story of the Sony Walkman*. London: SAGE.

Duguay, Stefanie. 2018. "Social Media's Breaking News: The Logic of Automation in Facebook Trending Topics and Twitter Moments." *Media International Australia* 166(1): 20–33.

Efrati, Amir. 2011. "Twitter Will Get 'Tweet' Trademark, Settles Lawsuit." *Wall Street Journal*, 10 October. https://blogs.wsj.com.

Florini, Sarah. 2014. "Tweets, Tweeps, and Signifyin': Communication and Cultural Performance on 'Black Twitter.'" *Television & New Media* 15(3): 223–237.

Freelon, Deen G., Charlton D. McIlwain, and Meredith D. Clark. 2016. "Beyond the Hashtags: #Ferguson, #Blacklivesmatter, and the Online Struggle for Offline Justice." Available at SSRN: http://dx.doi.org/10.2139/ssrn.2747066.

Galloway, Alexander R. 2004. *Protocol: How Control Exists after Decentralization*. Cambridge, MA: MIT Press.

Gannes, Liz. 2010. "The Short and Illustrious History of Twitter #Hashtags." *Gigaom*, 30 April. http://gigaom.com.

Gerlitz, Carolin, and Anne Helmond. 2013. "The 'Like' Economy: Social Buttons and the Data-Intensive Web." *New Media & Society* 15(8): 1348–1365.

Gibbs, Martin, James Meese, Michael Arnold, Bjorn Nansen, and Marcus Carter. 2015. "#Funeral and Instagram: Death, Social Media, and Platform Vernacular." *Information, Communication & Society* 18(3): 255–268.

Gillespie, Tarleton. 2014. "The Relevance of Algorithms." In Tarleton Gillespie, Pablo Boczkowski, and Kirsten Foot, eds., *Media Technologies: Essays on Communication, Materiality, and Society* (pp. 167–194). Cambridge, MA: MIT Press.

Glaser, Mark. 2007. "Your Guide to Micro-Blogging and Twitter." *Mediashift*, 15 May. http://mediashift.org.

Grigonis, Hillary. 2018. "As Twitter Cleans Up Spam, Monthly Users Drop, but Daily Engagement Increases." *Digital Trends*, 27 July. www.digitaltrends.com.

Halavais, Alex. 2014. "Structure of Twitter: Social and Technical." In Katrin Weller et al., eds., *Twitter and Society* (pp. 29–41). New York: Peter Lang.

Hallinan, Blake, and Ted Striphas. 2016. "Recommended for You: The Netflix Prize and the Production of Algorithmic Culture." *New Media & Society* 18(1): 117–137.

Harvey, Del, and David Gasca. 2018. "Serving Healthy Conversation." *Twitter Blog*, 15 May. https://blog.twitter.com.

Hartley, John, Jean Burgess, and Joshua Green. 2007. "'Laughs and Legends' or the Furniture That Glows? Television as History." *Australian Cultural History* 26: 15–36.

Helmond, Anne, David B. Nieborg, and Fernando N. van der Vlist. 2019. "Facebook's Evolution: Development of a Platform-as-Infrastructure." *Internet Histories* 3(2): 123–146. DOI: 10.1080/24701475.2019.1593667.

Henshaw-Plath, Evan. 2012. "Origin of the @reply—Digging through Twitter's History." *Anarchogeek*, 9 July. http://anarchogeek.com.

Honeycutt, Courtenay, and Susan C. Herring. 2009. "Beyond Microblogging: Conversation and Collaboration via Twitter." *42nd Hawaii International Conference on System Sciences*. IEEE. DOI: 10.1109/HICSS.2009.89.

Howard, Philip N., Samuel Woolley, and Ryan Calo. 2018. "Algorithms, Bots, and Political Communication in the US 2016 Election: The Challenge of

Automated Political Communication for Election Law and Administration." *Journal of Information Technology & Politics* 15(2): 81–93.

Joy, Jody. 2009. "Reinvigorating Object Biography: Reproducing the Drama of Object Lives." *World Archaeology* 41(4): 540–556.

Kelly, Ryan. 2009. "Twitter Study Reveals Interesting Results about Usage—40% Is Pointless Babble." *Pear Analytics Blog*, 12 August. http://pearanalytics.com.

Kennedy, Jenny, James Meese, and Emily van der Nagel. 2016. "Regulation and Social Practice Online." *Continuum: Journal of Media & Cultural Studies* 30(2): 146–157.

Khan, Imad. 2015. "Twitter Is Allowing Users to Claim Copyright Infringement on Tweets." *Daily Dot*, 25 July. www.dailydot.com.

Kooti, Farshad, Haeryun Yang, Meeyoung Cha, Krishna P. Gummadi, and Winter A. Mason. 2012. "The Emergence of Conventions in Online Social Networks." *International AAAI Conference on Weblogs and Social Media.* www.aaai.org/ocs/index.php/ICWSM/ICWSM12/paper/view/4661.

Kopytoff, Igor. 1988. "The Cultural Biography of Things." In Arjun Appadurai, ed., *The Social Life of Things: Commodities in Cultural Perspective* (pp. 64–91). Cambridge: Cambridge University Press.

Kottke, Jason. 2007. "Twitter vs Blogger Redux." *Kottke.org*, 11 May. https://kottke.org.

Lafrance, Adrienne, and Robinson Meyer. 2014. "A Eulogy for Twitter." *Atlantic*, 30 April. www.theatlantic.com.

Lu, Jessica H., and Catherine Knight Steele. 2019. "'Joy Is Resistance': Cross-Platform Resilience and (Re)invention of Black Oral Culture Online." *Information, Communication & Society* 22(6): 823–837. DOI: 10.1080/1369118X.2019.1575449.

Madianou, Mirca, and Daniel Miller. 2012. "Polymedia: Towards a New Theory of Digital Media in Interpersonal Communication." *International Journal of Cultural Studies*, 16(2): 169–187.

Marwick, Alice, and danah boyd. 2011. "I Tweet Honestly, I Tweet Passionately: Twitter Users, Context Collapse, and the Imagined Audience." *New Media and Society* 13(1): 114–133.

Marlow, Cameron, Mor Naaman, danah boyd, and Marc Davis. 2006. "HT06, Tagging Paper, Taxonomy, Flickr, Academic Article, To Read." *Proceedings of the Seventeenth Conference on Hypertext and Hypermedia* (pp. 31–40). ACM.

References

McGregor, Shannon C., and Logan Molyneux. 2018. "Twitter's Influence on News Judgment: An Experiment among Journalists." *Journalism*. DOI: 10.1177/1464884918802975.

McVeigh-Schultz, Joshua, and Nancy K. Baym. 2015. "Thinking of You: Vernacular Affordance in the Context of the Microsocial Relationship App, Couple." *Social Media + Society* 1(2). DOI: 10.1177/2056305115604649.

Messina, Chris. 2007a. "Groups for Twitter; or A Proposal for Twitter Tag Channels." *Factory Joe*, 25 August. http://factoryjoe.com.

———. 2007b. "Twitter Hashtags for Emergency Coordination and Disaster Relief." *Factory Joe*, 22 October. http://factoryjoe.com.

Meyer, Eric A. 2007. "The Twitters." *Meyerweb*, 21 January. http://meyerweb.com.

Miller, Claire C. 2009. "Twitter Serves Up Ideas from Its Followers." *New York Times*, 25 October. www.nytimes.com.

Monk-Payton, Brandy. 2017. "#Laughingwhileblack: Gender and the Comedy of Social Media Blackness." *Feminist Media Histories* 3(2): 15–35.

Murray, Garrett. 2012. "The Real History of the @reply on Twitter." *Maniacal Rage*, 10 July. http://log.maniacalrage.net.

Murthy, Dhiraj. 2012. *Twitter: Social Communication in the Digital Age*. 1st edition. Cambridge: Polity Press.

———. 2018. *Twitter: Social Communication in the Digital Age*. 2nd edition. Cambridge: Polity Press.

Musgrave, Shawn. 2017. "The Secret Twitter Rooms of Trump Nation." *Politico*, 9 August. www.politico.eu.

Needleman, Rafe. 2007. "Newbie's Guide to Twitter." *CNET*, 20 March. www.cnet.com.

Neff, Gina, and David Stark. 2003. "Permanently Beta: Responsive Organization in the Internet Era." In Philip N. Howard and Steve Jones, eds., *Society Online: The Internet in Context* (pp. 173–188). London: SAGE.

Notopoulos, Katie. 2013. "The Latest Twitter Trend: Manual Retweet Shaming." *BuzzFeed News*, 22 April. www.buzzfeed.com.

Papacharissi, Zizi. 2015. *Affective Publics: Sentiment, Technology, and Politics*. Oxford: Oxford University Press.

Papacharissi, Zizi, and Emily Easton. 2013. "In the Habitus of the New: Structure, Agency, and the Social Media Habitus." In John Hartley, Jean Burgess, and Axel Bruns, eds., *A Companion to New Media Dynamics* (pp. 167–184). London: Wiley-Blackwell.

Parr, Ben. 2009a. "#FixReplies Controversy: Users Want @reply Options Back." *Mashable*, 13 May. http://mashable.com.

———. 2009b. "HOW TO: Retweet on Twitter." *Mashable*, 16 April. http://mashable.com

Paßmann, Johannes, Thomas Boeschoten, and Mirko T. Schäfer. 2014. "The Gift of the Gab: Retweet Cartels and Gift Economies on Twitter." In Katrin Weller et al., eds., *Twitter and Society* (pp. 331–344). New York: Peter Lang.

Pinch, Trevor J., and Wiebe E. Bijker. 1984. "The Social Construction of Facts and Artefacts: Or How the Sociology of Science and the Sociology of Technology Might Benefit Each Other." *Social Studies of Science* 14(3): 399–441.

Postigo, Hector. 2016. "The Socio-technical Architecture of Digital Labor: Converting Play into YouTube Money." *New Media & Society* 8(2): 332–349.

Rambukkana, Nathan. 2015. *Hashtag Publics: The Power and Politics of Discursive Networks*. New York: Peter Lang.

Rao, Leena. 2009. "Twitter Makes Hashtags More #Useful." *Techcrunch*, 2 July. http://techcrunch.com

Reichelt, Lisa. 2007. "Ambient Intimacy." *Disambiguity*, 1 March. www.disambiguity.com

Rogers, Richard. 2014. "Debanalizing Twitter: The Transformation of an Object of Study." In Katrin Weller et al., eds., *Twitter and Society* (pp. ix–xxvi). New York: Peter Lang.

Sagolla, Dom. 2012. "First Use of Twitter @ Sign." *140 Characters*, 6 June. www.140characters.com.

Serres, Michael. 1995. *Genesis*. Ann Arbor: University of Michigan Press.

Sherman, Todd. 2016. "Coming Soon: Express Even More in 140 Characters." *Twitter Blog*, 24 May. https://blog.twitter.com.

Shu, Catherine. 2015. "Twitter Officially Launches Its 'Retweet with Comment' Feature." *Techcrunch*, 6 April. http://techcrunch.com.

Sniderman, Zachary. 2010. "The Origin of Twitter's 'Fail Whale.'" *Mashable*, 2 August. https://mashable.com.

Stocks, Karen. 2016. "Twitter Turns 10." *Twitter Blog*, 20 March. https://blog.twitter.com.

Stone, Biz. 2007. "Are You Twittering @ Me?" *Twitter Blog*, 30 May. https://blog.twitter.com.

References

———. 2009a. "The Replies Kerfuffle." *Twitter Blog*, 14 May. https://blog. twitter.com.

———. 2009b. "What's Happening?" *Twitter Blog*, 19 November. https://blog. twitter.com.

———. 2009c. "Project Retweet: Phase One." *Twitter Blog*, 13 August. https:// blog.twitter.com.

Sweet, Melissa, Luke Pearson, and Pat Dudgeon. 2013. "@IndigenousX: A Case Study of Community-Led Innovation in Digital Media." *Media International Australia* 149(1): 104–111.

Trice, Michael, and Liza Potts. 2018. "Building Dark Patterns into Platforms: How GamerGate Perturbed Twitter's User Experience." *Present Tense: A Journal of Rhetoric in Society* 6: 3. www.presenttensejournal.org.

Twitter. 2017. "Twitter—Company," 21 April. https://about.twitter.com.

Ulanoff, Lance. 2014. "Is Twitter Getting Rid of @-Replies and Hashtags?" *Mashable*, 20 March. http://mashable.com.

van Dijck, José. 2013. *Culture of Connectivity: A Critical History of Social Media*. New York: Oxford University Press. Kindle.

van Dijck, José, and Thomas Poell. 2013. "Understanding Social Media Logic." *Media and Communication* 1(1). 2–14.

Vieweg, Sarah, Amanda L. Hughes, Kate Starbird, and Leysia Palen. 2010. "Microblogging during Two Natural Hazards Events: What Twitter May Contribute to Situational Awareness." *Proceedings of the SIGCHI Conference on Human Factors in Computing Systems* (pp. 1079–1088). ACM.

Weller, Katrin, Axel Bruns, Jean Burgess, Merja Mahrt, and Cornelius Puschmann, eds. 2014. *Twitter and Society*. New York: Peter Lang.

Whitlock, Tim. 2010. "Old vs New Retweets and Why I Made the RT Button." *Timwhitlock.info*, 4 October. https://timwhitlock.info.

Williams, Evan. 2009. "Why Retweet Works the Way It Does." *Evhead*, 10 November. http://evhead.com (archived at http://web.archive.org).

Williams, Raymond. 1974. *Television: Technology and Cultural Form*. London: Routledge.

Zara, Christopher. 2018. "Twitter's User Growth Just Took a Big Hit." *Fast Company*, 27 July. www.fastcompany.com.

Zittrain, Jonathan. 2008. *The Future of the Internet—and How to Stop It*. New Haven, CT: Yale University Press.

Index

power: centralization of, 24; of features, 34–35; of joy and balanced communication, 116

professional networking, 47

programmability, 21

protocological objects, 34

public oversight, 16

public pedagogy: emergence of, 8; around RT feature, 85

public relations tool, 4

Rambukkana, Nathan, 67

relationships: Twitter's with third-party developers, 10–11; users' social, 27–28

replies, 45–58

Replies Kerfuffle post, 55–56

retweet cartels, 102

retweet (RT) feature: for activism, 96–97; alternatives to, 84–86; appropriation of, 83–87; for community participation, 95–96; competition, 94–95; concept sketch of, 88, 88; contestation of, 97–105; Facebook similarities to, 98; for humor, 93–94; incorporation of, 87–97, 88; integrity issues addressed with, 89–90, 104; iteration of, 105–6; journalists using, 93; manual RTs and, 99–100, 101, 103; official announcement of, 87–89, 88; organic retweeting and, 92; public pedagogy around, 85; purpose of, 83; with quotes, 90, 105–6, 123n26; self-censoring with, 103; social norms around, 85–86; Stone on, 87–89; track-

ability, 91; username syntax and, 91–92; Williams on, 90–91

rituals, 71–72

Rogers, Richard, 22

RT feature. *See* retweet feature

Sagolla, Dom, 41, 121n2

San Diego brushfires, 63–64

Scandal, 72

search.twitter.com, 66

second screen tweeting, 72–73

self-censoring, 103

shaming, 99

sketches, concept: of RT feature, 88, 88; for status update-based social network, 4, 5

smartphones: permanent beta and continuous updating for, 25; Zittrain concerned with, 24

sociability, 115

social churning, 25

social lives, 27

Social Media Collective blog, 30

social media logics, 20–21

social media platforms: coming of age narrative for, 21–22; culture of connectivity across, 20; elements of, 16–17; # feature used across, 61–62; hope for, 115–16; platform biography approach for, 16, 26–32, 109, 113–16; public oversight of, 16; studying, 15–26; tension between generativity and usability for, 115; user interfaces as culture of, 33–34; Van Dijck on diagnosing, 24; vernaculars of, 30. *See also* features; *specific platforms*

About the Authors

Jean Burgess is Professor in the School of Communication and Director of the Digital Media Research Centre at Queensland University of Technology, Australia. In addition to 120 other scholarly outputs, she is co-author or editor of five previous books on digital media, communication, and culture.

Nancy K. Baym is Senior Principal Researcher at Microsoft in Cambridge, Massachusetts. She is the author and co-editor of five previous books about communication, relationships, and the internet. More information, most of her articles, and some of her talks are available at nancybaym.com.